This Is From Me

Audrey J Shrive

by

Audrey Joy Shrive

Scripture taken from the New American Standard Bible Copyright © 1960, 1962, 1963, 1968, 1971, 1972, 1973, 1975, 1977 by The Lockman Foundation. Used by permission.

Contact the publisher and/or author at: ThisIsFromMe2020@gmail.com

Credits:
Cover Design, Layout, Editing by Alane Pearce, Professional Writing Services.
Cover Images: Woman - ava-sol-rvGKp2U0834-unsplash; clouds in sky - rafael-garcin-mOLUAnslHmw-unsplash; man walking away - Padli Pradana - pexels

Publishing coaching, and project management by Alane Pearce, Professional Writing Services.
Contact Alane at APearceWriting@gmail.com

Shrive, Audrey Joy: This Is From Me
    1. Memoir   2. Christian Living   3. Alcholosim

This book is dedicated to my friend, Major Jason Paxton. He was a dedicated soldier who saw and experienced more than he could bear.

Acknowledgements

I want to thank my parents for raising me to be the person I am today. They are hard-working, honest people and raised their four children to be the same. I was blessed to have grown up in a Christian home.

Thank you to my siblings, Jerry, Peggy, and Patrick who supported me each in their own way as I went through my divorce and in the writing of this book.

Thanks for the listening, love and support given by my friends Gina, Pam, Vern, Dave, and Marilyn as I walked through the beginning of this mess.

Thank you to my friend Alane, who first planted the seed to write this book and then helped me get it across the finish line.

Thank you to my husband for letting me pursue my lifelong dream to 'just write'. The fact that it's concluded in a published book is icing on the cake.

Above all, thank you to God for His provision, protection, and healing.

Prologue

"Pain is the difference between what is
and what I want it to be."
The Precious Present

I sat down in my living room chair. The big pink and blue swivel recliner was so comfortable it felt like a hug every time I sat in it. This is where I had my quiet time each morning. This is where I watched TV in the evenings. The sun shone through the window in front of me giving a soft glow to the hardwood floors of the military housing unit that was home for us at Ft. Bragg in Fayettville, North Carolina. It was a warm and humid May day in 1997.

I was exhausted, having barely slept the last several nights. If ever I had needed a hug and the comfort of friends, it was today. I wiped the tears from my eyes, took a deep breath and dialed the number of my friend and former co-worker, Becky. Her husband Bruce answered the phone.

"Bruce here," he said.

"Hi Bruce, this is Audrey," I responded.

"Audrey! How are things?" he asked

"Well Bruce, things are not as I expected them to be," I answered. "Is Becky there?"

Chapter One
From The Cradle To Colorado

"If at first you succeed, hide your astonishment."
(Bill Griffith)

Little Auddy

I learned to drive when I was three years old. Well, sort of. I grew up on a 900-acre irrigated farm and ranch in Fall River County, South Dakota. Fall River is the most south and west county in the state. It's bordered by Wyoming to the west and Nebraska to the south. Dad ran about 150 head of cattle in what is called a cow/calf operation. This means he bred the heifers each year and then sold the calves when they became of marketable age, usually at around one year. In the winter months, the cattle were brought in from pasture to be closer to our home for a couple of reasons; they would calve in February, and it was easier to feed them. To accomplish the feeding task, Dad sometimes needed help. Cattlemen and farmers are resourceful problem solvers. Dad's solution when he was short on proper help was to put me behind the wheel of his pick-up.

Dad loaded the necessary hay bales for the evening feed in the back of the truck. He drove us to the cattle pasture, put the truck in neutral, and stood me on the driver's side behind the wheel. I knew left and right, so he gave me direction to listen to his instruction, then slightly turn the wheel left and right as he told me. Never was the vehicle going faster than 1 or 2 mph. Should anything have gone awry, which it never did, he could have covered the ground from the back of the pick-up to the cab with no problem. While he heaved hay bales to the hungry cattle, he would call out from time-to-time, using his pet name for me, "A little to the right, Auddy. Okay, now a little to the left."

Dad was born and raised in Fall River County. His grandparents homesteaded there in 1883. At the writing of this book, the homestead is still in our family. My mother was born and raised in Alabama, near Birmingham. She came to teach the children of missionaries at a Native American Mission in Fall River County in 1960. She taught at that school two years, and then began teaching at a little country school in the community of Oral, South Dakota. Oral is where Dad and his family lived. Mom became acquainted with the family of another teacher at the Oral school. She met Dad through this family after Dad's wife passed away. They were married on April 14th, 1963. I came along, one year, one week and one day later. They didn't waste any time!

I was born into a world of adults. Dad had two children from his first marriage. My brother, Jerry, is 15 years older than me. My sister, Peggy, is 12 years older. In the summer months, there was a small army of hired help that moved into our little house.

There was much to be done to plant, irrigate and then harvest the alfalfa hay and corn our farm grew. Mom's job was to keep them all fed and their clothes clean. Not easy with a baby. Three years later, my brother Patrick rounded out the family. Jerry went to college when I was three – thus the need for my early driving lessons. Peggy departed for college when I was six. Therefore, even as a middle child, I have all the traits of the eldest sibling. Since I was accustomed to having so many adults willing to address my every need, I thought the world revolved around me. I'm sure my parents didn't mean for it to happen. It's just I'm pretty persistent and if one person wouldn't read to me or play with me, I found one who would.

When I started first grade (we didn't have kindergarten at the little country school in Oral), I was stunned to learn the other kids had no interest in doing what I told them to do. It was so bad, I got an F in 'getting along with others' in the second grade. I do recall there was a very intense conversation between my mother and the teacher out in the cloakroom the day after report cards came home. Being a teacher herself, Mom really thought the teacher should have let her and Dad know there was a problem so they could work with me to improve the issue, verses having an F on my report card. Being a high achiever from a young age, I was pretty motivated to figure out how to avoid that sort of thing in the future. I don't remember what 'education' was given me about how to treat people, but am sure there were several age-appropriate conversations. That said, I'm still bossy. I was the de facto eldest child after all.

When I was in third grade, Dad opened a real estate office in town. "Town" was Hot Springs, South Dakota, about 25 miles away from Oral. Dad had a hired man to help run the farm and ranch. In addition, my brother Jerry and sister Peggy had moved back to the area. They, along with their spouses, had similar operations to Dad's, all within a five-mile radius. Everyone worked together to get the work done at each other's places. Because Mom and Dad were in town every day to operate the real estate office, Patrick and I were enrolled in school in Hot Springs. No more little country school. Now there were 90 kids in my grade, where before there were only two of us! What a culture shock that was for me.

The other monumental thing that happened to me at age nine, was I accepted Christ. I had a Sunday school teacher who led us in the sinners' prayer at the end of each class. I was stubborn. I was just NOT going to do that because the teacher said so. Then, brother Jerry got saved. He came to tell Mom and Dad about the experience. I remember sitting at the kitchen table, eating my breakfast one morning and listening to this conversation. It made a huge impression on me because I thought Jerry walked on water already. You would think that would be enough for me to say the sinner's prayer in Sunday school the next Sunday, but no. I was going to do it my way, in my time. That Sunday afternoon, while everyone was napping, I got my Children's Living Bible out and tried to find a passage of meaning. Not being much of a nine-year-old savant Bible scholar, I really had no idea what I was looking for or doing. I finally just started talking to God.

"Dear Jesus," I said, "Miss Adams says I need to accept you as my Lord and Savior. I didn't know about that, but now that Jerry has done it, I suppose I need to take this seriously. I think I'm supposed to ask you into my heart. So, I would like to do that now. Thank you. Amen."

Not much of a sinner's prayer, but hey, I was nine.

Being nine also meant Mom could enroll me in 4-H. There was a club in Oral and I became a part of it. I joined in the fall and within a few months Mom entered me in the Demonstration Days competition. I gave my first speech at age nine on how to make bookmarks from felt and decorate them. I'd never felt 'nervous' before, but as I gave my talk, I remember my skinny little legs and ankles shaking so hard I was sure everyone in the audience could see. I got a blue ribbon. The highest ribbon in 4-H is purple, the next is blue, then red, then white. I never got a white ribbon and only one red in my 10-year career as a 4-Her. Well, I almost got a red ribbon, I should say.

4-H members have projects. My projects included, photography, sewing, speaking, showing livestock, home improvement, and cooking. When I was 14, I signed up to enter peanut butter cookies into the county fair. I later changed my mind and decided to enter chocolate chip cookies. I called the extension office to tell them I would be entering a different type of cookie. The extension agent told me she would make the change on my entry. Well, she didn't. At the county fair judging, while the judges very much liked my chocolate chip cookies, they gave me a red ribbon because the entry was 'wrong.' I pled my case with the judges, then the extension agent. She had no memory of the phone call. So, I removed my entry. There was no way I was going to let my good name be reflected poorly due to someone else's failure to do their job. I took my cookies and left.

Mom was informed of what I'd done and after a few minutes, she came to find me, give me the 'good sport' talk and convince me to re-enter the cookies in question.

"Mom," I said, "I will not be embarrassed by having a red ribbon next to my name when it's not my mistake. Besides, I already ate the cookies."

I knew I was golden when I saw Mom fight to hide the smile that almost crossed her face and choke a bit on the laugh that almost escaped her mouth. She did what every good parent does in that moment and held it in, although I overheard her and Dad having a pretty good chuckle over it later. Besides, she knew I was right.

Solid Foundation

Going to a small high school meant I was involved in a lot of activities. I was in band, ran track, and was a cheerleader all through school, on top of my 4-H activities. Not only that, like any farm kid, I had responsibilities at home. Before and after school our 4-H livestock had to be fed and watered, and I was responsible for the chickens. The chickens had to be fed and watered. Also, the eggs had to be gathered every afternoon. I got to sell the eggs our family didn't eat. They sold for a dollar a dozen and I usually brought in about five dollars a week. By the time I was a senior in high school, I was over it. I didn't want the chickens or the money they brought. I had a job in town on Saturdays and I would be leaving for college in just a few months. I knew I couldn't just announce I was done. I had to figure a way to convince Dad to take that responsibility away from me.

I approached him one day and said, "Dad, it's my understanding the chickens are intended to teach me responsibility, is that right?"

"Yes," Dad replied.

"Do you think I'm a responsible young person?" I asked.

"Yah. You do pretty well in that department," he answered.

"Well then, can we get rid of the darn chickens?" I asked.

Dad chuckled a bit, reminded me I would be losing the egg money and then conceded. The one condition was that I helped him butcher and dress them. I agreed to his terms and the next weekend the great chicken massacre took place. We've all heard the phrase 'running around like a chicken with their head cut off'...so, that's a real thing. We were in the chicken coup. When we got to the place where there were three chickens running around with their head cut off, and I knew there were about 27 more to go, I stepped out telling Dad to let me know when he was done. I would help him pluck and dress these fowl birds, but that crazy sight was more than I could handle.

I also worked on the school newspaper all four years of high school. This was one of my favorite activities. I enjoyed interviewing people for the story and I genuinely loved writing the story. I had a knack for it and in fact, worked on college newspapers throughout my college career.

Part of my responsibilities on the high school paper was to sell advertising space. This was my introduction into sales. I didn't have much of a sales pitch, but I was sincere in my efforts. I always dressed in business attire when I went out selling to the local business owners. This made a statement. Mom taught me that. Also, I never assumed a business owner would buy ads in the high school paper. I approached them with respect. Dad taught me that.

I started dabbling in pageants at age 14 and went on to compete in the Miss South Dakota pageant in 1987 as Miss Fall River. It was such an honor to represent my home county, in my hometown as the pageant was held in Hot Springs at the time. Pageants get criticism today, but I gained a ton of self-confidence because of those competitions. A valuable skill that pageants taught me was how to do a panel interview. I've had a few of those in my career and had it not been for pageants, I likely would have failed that test miserably and not gotten the job.

In rural states like South Dakota, farm kids can get a learner's permit to drive when they're fourteen. That means they are on the road for two full years before getting an official driver's license. They don't have to have an adult with them and are free to drive during daylight hours or to and from school or school functions. Dad bought me a used 1970, avocado green, Dodge Dart to drive. This meant I didn't have to take the bus to school anymore and could get an entire 30 minutes more sleep in the mornings! I started driving Patrick to school when I was a freshman in high school. I drove on all kinds of roads in all kinds of conditions. Dad did a good job of teaching us how to drive in mud, ice, snow, and rain. This skill would come in handy later.

College Chaos

I graduated from high school in 1982. I wasn't sure what I wanted to study, so I spent my first two years at Chadron State College in Chadron, Nebraska. I was in band, jazz band, wrote for the school paper and was a cheerleader my sophomore year.

I was a virgin when I went to college. As a Christian, I was proud of this. The boys knew I didn't 'put out'. In fact, just before graduation, as a joke, a couple of students made a list of who among the classmates were virgins. My name was third on the list. While I wasn't very popular, my classmates knew my values.

On October 4, 1982, my virginity was taken from me in a date rape situation. I was devastated. I felt so ruined and humiliated. I didn't tell a soul what happened to me for a really long time. I was sure it was my fault somehow for being where I shouldn't have been, alone in a boy's dorm room with said boy. Years later I was watching a movie that focused on the topic of date rape. I'd never heard the phrase. I distinctly remember saying out loud to myself, "That's what happened to me. It has a name." Knowing that other women had experienced what I had was validating.

The loss of my virginity in a way that was not at all what I intended, sent me down a path of living in rebellion and debauchery. I was saving my virginity for marriage. When that was robbed from me, I believed satan's lie that I was no longer pure, so I reasoned that I might as well do whatever felt good. I drew the line at drugs. I was terrified of drugs. I grew up in the era of Nancy Reagan's anti-drug campaign and can still hear the sizzle of the egg being dropped in the frying pan after the statement, "This is your brain." (Egg drop) "This is your brain on drugs."

Instead of drugs, I started drinking and going to parties. I became sexually promiscuous. My heart was hard and my mouth was foul. I wasn't very comfortable being a 'bad girl', but once you go down that path it's hard to turn around. I somehow always seemed to stay just a bit ahead of disaster. I now believe that was God keeping me alive and protecting me from my own stupidity.

During my time at Chadron State I figured out I wanted to major in Mass Communications with an emphasis on Broadcast Media. Chadron didn't have this course of study, so my junior year I transferred to the University of South Dakota (USD). USD is in Vermillion, South Dakota. I spent three years at USD and ultimately came away with two degrees; Mass Communication and English. I settled down a little bit at USD, but not much. I didn't participate in many extra-curricular activities, as I really wanted to focus on my major. I did write for the school paper and my last year there was the assistant editor. I was also a DJ at the local radio station for two years.

During that time, God never stopped pursuing me. In quiet moments, usually in the early hours after a night of partying, I could hear that still, small voice gently say, "Come back to me."

"I'm not ready yet God," I would answer.

"That's okay," He'd say. "I'll be here when you're ready."

I knew I was living a sinners' lifestyle. When I was home and went to church with my parents, if it happened to be communion Sunday, I would refuse communion. I was convinced I'd bring worse judgment on myself if I took communion without repenting. Somewhere along the line I'd heard a teaching or a sermon on I Corinthians 11: 27-29.

> *"Therefore whoever eats the bread or drinks the cup of the Lord in an unworthy manner, shall be guilty of the body and the blood of the Lord. But let a man examine himself, and so let him eat of the bread and drink of the cup. For he who eats and drinks, eats and drinks judgment to himself, if he does not judge the body rightly."*

I understood these verses to mean I needed to confess and repent, which means to change my direction. I wasn't ready to repent, but I did take this scripture seriously. I was already in trouble with God and out of right relationship with him. By God's unmerited grace, I never had anything worse happen to me in those years other than a couple of broken hearts doled out by guys I thought I loved.

I did have a few adventures driving home from USD to see Mom and Dad for the weekend. They provided a vehicle for me to drive so I could get home from time to time. They sent me off to USD with a 1980 Dodge Aspen. It was brown in color and the only drawback was it had no AC. It was a cute car and I was proud to drive it. In the fall of 1986, Dad decided to move vehicles around. My grandmother, who lived in Alabama, bought a new car. Dad wanted to use the Dodge Aspen as a trade for a new pickup, so he bought Granny's car for me. It was a 1970 Dodge Cornet. It had a 30-gallon tank. Gas was $2.00 a gallon. I could barely afford to put gas in it. It weighed over three thousand pounds--one and a half tons! My cool factor went way down, but the price was right. Dad delivered it to me in October and told me he'd get snow tires on it when I came home for Thanksgiving.

Of course, a snowstorm moved across South Dakota the day I was heading home for Thanksgiving break. Mom, Dad, and I talked it over and decided it would be best for me to travel on the interstate, verses the southern route on state highways I preferred to drive from Vermillion. The plan was I would drive an hour north to Sioux Falls, travel west on I-25 to Rapid City, then an hour south to home. This changed a 400-mile trip to a 500-mile trip, but there are more towns along I-25 and the road is more travelled. The folks knew if I got into car trouble of some sort, ready help was more likely. Plus, I was going to caravan with another student from Hot Springs. Once the roads became bad, I had to slow to a crawl because of my tires. Before long, my travel buddy gave up on me and left me to fend for myself.

Hours later, about 100 miles east of Rapid City, I came across her car in the ditch. She was nowhere to be seen. I saw what I presumed to be a farm light to the north. Thinking she might have walked there for help, I took the exit and drove to the light.

When I pulled in I realized this was not at all a farmhouse, it was a missile silo attached to Ellsworth Air Force base. Inside were nuclear weapons! Since I was basically trespassing on Federal land, I wanted to get out of there as quickly as possible. There was just one problem though, my car's front tires were in the tiniest of dips. The snow was packed and slick. I was stuck. I tried everything I could think of to get unstuck. I ground up some corn chips and packed them under the back tires. No luck. I was travelling with a dog, whom I tried to coax onto the gas pedal so I could push. It's probably a good thing that didn't work out. I didn't think that idea all the way through.

Finally, I did what I'd seen my dad do in this type of situation many times. I started 'rocking' the car by moving from reverse to drive and pushing with my left leg out of the door. It might have worked. I will never know. I looked up from my efforts to see six airmen standing at parade rest watching me. I threw the car in park, jumped out and hollered, "Man, am I glad to see you boys! I'm stuck. Would you mind terribly giving me a wee bit of a push?"

What they didn't know is that I didn't have snow tires, so they thought I was super stuck. None of them spoke. They moved in unison to the front of my car and put everything they had into it. The car really could have been moved with one finger in all likelihood. All six men fell face down on the ground as soon as the car moved. I rolled down my window as I drove out and hollered my thanks as they brushed themselves off.

I continued on my way and finally made it home around midnight. I was on the road 12 hours for what normally would have been a 9-hour drive. Oh, and my friend hitched a ride with a trucker. She got a tongue wagging from me the next morning for leaving me behind, driving too fast for the conditions and hitch-hiking!

As for me, I ruined the transmission 'rocking' the car. Dad didn't have much to say about that. He admitted we probably should have gotten snow tires sooner, but it all worked out in the end.

As I mentioned, the drive from Vermillion home was about 400 miles if I took southern state highways. It was the quickest and most direct route and that's how I usually travelled when the roads weren't bad. I often stopped at a gas station in Martin, South Dakota to empty out, fill up and stretch a bit. The next spring, I came home for Easter and used this route. When I arrived in Martin and pulled into my favorite gas station, I observed the state road in front of me was mud for as far as I could see. When I say mud, I mean deep, thick, black clay that was no joke. After I had done my business, I asked the attendant, "How far is the road muddy like this?"

"Oh, about seven miles," he replied.

"Is *anyone* driving it?" I asked.

"Nope. Not without four-wheeled drive," he answered matter-of-factly.

I went to the pay phone and tried to reach my parents. I called the office in town. No answer. It was after five and everyone was gone for the day. I called home. No answer. They weren't home yet. I called my brother Jerry's house. No answer. Called my sister Peggy's house. No answer. Answering machines were just coming into common use and no one in my family had one yet.

I wanted to take a different route, but really wanted someone to know. I could travel south into Nebraska, or north up to I-25, but this would add a couple of hours to my trip. If something happened to me like a wreck or if I encountered mud like this on a back road and got stuck, my parents would have no way of knowing where I was. I reasoned the best course of action was to go the way they thought I would. If I got stuck, and didn't arrive home when expected, they would come looking for me. Besides, thanks to Dad's excellent driving training and years of living on a dirt road, I was really good at driving in mud. I had good tires now, and my car weighed over a ton. I felt sure I could make it.

The idea of waiting where I was until I could get in touch with my parents and come up with a plan together crossed my mind, but only for a second. I'm my father's daughter and patience is not my strong suit. I can do anything better than wait.

So, I put my big girl panties on, took a deep breath and said, "You can do this Audrey."

The key to driving in mud is to keep a somewhat slow and steady speed. I waded into the muddy Martin mess, hit a good steady stride, and went. The good news was there was no one else on the road, so I could take my half down the middle. There was some slipping and sliding, but I was holding my own and gaining confidence with each mile.

Then I came over a hill to see a car almost in the ditch on the left side of the road and five or six people standing about. My first instinct was to brake, but I realized two things; if I stopped, I was through and, most importantly, none of the people were in my way. They were at the bottom of the hill, milling around their stalled car. There was a good-sized hill on the other side I needed to crest. So, I did the opposite. I pressed the gas and went right on by them. A couple of them were closer to the middle of the road. They started running towards the ditch and I'm pretty sure I saw one guy dive into the ditch head first to be sure he was out of my way. When I got to the bottom of the hill, I found what had derailed their car. I hit a bump so big that my head hit the car roof in the bounce, and that was with my seatbelt on.

Even so, I didn't slow down one bit. I kept my car in the road and topped the hill. Before long I was through the seven-mile mud and on a regular state highway.

When I pulled into the driveway at home, Dad looked at me and said, "What happened to your car?"

I explained and his eyes got big.

"Oops, I forgot to tell you about that," he said. "Why didn't you go around?" he asked.

I explained my thought process and at the end of the conversation, he agreed with my reasoning and felt I made the right decision.

Time to Adult

I finally completed my college course study in May of 1987. I went home for the summer to compete in the Miss South Dakota pageant. I didn't win the title, so it was time to get a job. My first job out of college was advertising sales for a radio station in Sioux City, Iowa. Sioux City is about 35 miles south of Vermillion. I loved the work, but was given a sales radius of 200 miles around Sioux City. They wanted to expand their market into rural areas and hired the farm girl to do it. Their experiment didn't work. I refused to sell to the rural implement dealers and feed and seed stores that were so far away from Sioux City. There would be no good return on investment for them. I really believed convincing these rural businesses to spend money on something that wouldn't yield results was unethical. They were better off spending a few hundred dollars with their local station, not the several thousand they would have needed to make a splash in the big city market.

I was the daughter of a small business owner in a small town in rural America who also happened to be a farmer and rancher. I was much more an expert on the subject than they were, but in their eyes, I was a kid right out of college who didn't know anything. I pled my case over and over and asked for a list in town. I was told no time and again. I've never been really clear if I quit or if I was fired, but I found myself without a job two weeks before Christmas.

Dad gave me one week to find a new job or I was going to have to move back home. I was one motivated gal. I found a job before the week was out, working with Junior Achievement (JA) in Sioux City. I started January 1st, 1988 and spent nearly four years there.

I held many positions within the small non-profit. I was charged with bringing in new donors and managing existing donors, handling all media communications and interviews, organizing fund raisers like bowling tournaments and golf tournaments and the best part, overseeing the kids programs. I totally loved the job and had a great deal of success in the work. I don't know why, but it surprised me some at how well I did. I came across this quote in a Reader's Digest magazine early in my time at JA. "If at first you succeed hide your astonishment." I cut it out I kept it on the bulletin board next to my desk. I still have it in my office today.

I also became great friends with one of my co-workers, Becky. She and her husband Bruce looked out for me. I think they felt since I was single and young, I needed help now and then. They were always who I would call in a pinch.

The headquarters for JA is in Colorado Springs, Colorado. I was sent there numerous times for training. I fell in love with Colorado Springs. The weather in Vermillion, South Dakota and Sioux City, Iowa left a lot to be desired in my mind. It was bitter cold and miserable in the winter months, and horribly hot and humid in the summer. Colorado Springs has the most moderate and mild climate year-round of anywhere I've ever been. The average temperature in the winter is 50 degrees and the low 80's in the summer. The falls are amazing! There's extremely low humidity in Colorado Springs. It does snow, but usually melts within a couple of days. No matter what time of year I visited the weather was fabulous!

Between the stellar weather, coupled with the amazing views of the Rockies and America's mountain, Pikes Peak, Colorado Springs had my heart from the get-go. I made up my mind that somehow, some way, someday I was going to move to Colorado Springs. I hoped to do that with JA. The idea of working at the national headquarters of Junior Achievement was very appealing to me.

My personal life was still a mess. I went from one bad dating situation to another. I told myself I was choosing to date guys I would never marry because I wasn't ready to get married. While there was some truth to this, I suspect I still saw myself as impure and ruined. I was sure the kind of guy I wanted would never want me. I was with one guy for a couple of years. As we spent time together, I figured out he was an alcoholic. I didn't know anything about alcoholism. I learned just enough to know I didn't like it. I also realized he was very depressed. I was concerned if I ended the relationship, he would take his own life.

I was growing weary of the life I was leading. I realized I needed help to turn things around. I found a church and began attending every Sunday. I really didn't know how to pray or how to have a quiet time but knew these were things I should be doing. I'd never really been discipled or taught how to exercise these disciplines. I decided I'd figure it out as I went. I picked up a devotional at church and began a daily quiet time. My way back to God was slow. I kept one foot in church and one foot in the world for a long time. Even so, I wanted out of this bad relationship in the worst way, but knew it needed to be his idea or it wouldn't go well. I prayed every day for a week that God would help me get out of the relationship.

The boyfriend came to me that Friday night and broke up with me. Go God! I should get an Academy Award for how sad and hurt I acted. The relief I felt to be rid of him was huge. Now, I could get on with my life and make better decisions. This would be slow in coming, but at least I was headed in the right direction.

In the fall of 1991, I was given an offer for my dream job at the Junior Achievement National Headquarters in Colorado Springs. The work was to plan the International Student Forum, a business conference for high school students from around the world. It was a great opportunity. My first day at work was November 9, 1991.

I had my dream job. I was living where I wanted to live. I found a church. Life was nearly perfect, except for one thing. I was alone. I was ready to find a husband. It was time to settle down.

Chapter 2
Meeting My Cowboy

"I hear there's a fine for harboring an angel."

He Two-Stepped Into My Heart

We did everything wrong. We met in a bar. Moved in together way to soon. We met in February and were engaged by August. We didn't put God first in the beginning. The one thing we did right was church. Still, we always used to joke that when we met; my walk with the Lord had a limp and his was completely lame.

It was a cold February night when Steve sauntered up to me in the local country watering hole, Cowboys, and asked me to dance. I looked up to see who was asking and saw the most serious, saddest blue eyes I'd ever seen. The black cowboy hat on his head added to the seriousness. He had on a bright striped brush popper shirt that was popular in the day, and his nylon belt stylishly hung down a few inches from the buckle. He took me by the hand and led me to the dance floor. The DJ was playing

George Strait's "The Cowboy Rides Away". He pulled me close and said, "Good song. Wrong theme, but good song."

We two-stepped around the dance floor, moving with the sea of other couples.

As that song ended and Mary Chapin Carpenter's, "Down at the Twist and Shout" came on. He spoke again. "Grab hold!" he commanded, as he transitioned from a gentle two step to a wild three step. He spun me around and around the dance floor. It was so fun!

And so, it began. I ran into him several times over the next few weeks at the same club. I can't really say we talked a lot. Steve's a 'still waters run deep' kind of guy. Since he wasn't much of a talker, we danced. One night we went home together. As he drove me back to the club to get my truck the next day, he looked at me and said, "I hear there's a fine for harboring an angel. Hope God doesn't get mad at me for hanging on to you."

That was the moment I began to fall in love. He started calling me every day after work, coming over to my apartment in the evenings and before either one of us really realized what had happened, he was living there.

Steve was in the Army. Colorado Springs is a military town. It's hard to meet any young single male who isn't active duty. Having no interest in being a military spouse, I only got serious about a future together after he told me he was getting out of the Army at the end of his current enlistment. The other thing that gave me pause was he told me he was an alcoholic. After my experience in Sioux City, I had no interest in going down that road again. When he told me this about himself, he also told me he was thinking of making some changes. He quit drinking two weeks after we met. Alcohol was not part of our dating experience after that.

We spent our weekends dancing at Cowboys on Friday or Saturday nights. On Sundays after church, we would drive to Pueblo West and later, to Penrose, Colorado so he could buck out. Steve was an aspiring bull rider and there was a guy who had 'practice' every Sunday afternoon all year long. After the buck out, we'd get a $5.00 steak and baked potato at Cowboys.

One Sunday afternoon he drew the bull to win, Captain Marvel. Now Marvel was the biggest bull in Dean Drake's stock. And he was mean. He also had only been ridden the full eight seconds once. It probably would have been a good decision for Steve not to ride Captain Marvel, but I maintain bull riders haven't had all of their brains grow in yet, so he tied on. He came out of the chute strong and then after two jumps everything went wrong in a hurry. Steve's riggin' came loose. He came off the bull going over the bull's head, just as the bull reared his head up. This catapulted Steve high in the air and shot him like a cannon toward the fence. He hit the fence so hard, he actually broke the 2x8 fence slab. He split it right down the middle.

Blood was running from his nose and his eye. The bull's head had collided with his nose. Marvel's horn cut open the corner of Steve's eye. The bull fighters and other cowboys carried Steve out of the arena and gave him an ice pack. I came out of the bleachers like I'd been poked with a hot shot and went full sprint to where they had him. There was no ambulance on site. It was practice after all. This cowboy needed a doctor and needed one now.

There were two problems. We were in his little Chevy S-10, which was a stick shift. Dad did teach me how to drive a stick, but I'm not at all good at it. The other problem was we were both new to the area and had no idea where the closest hospital was or how to get there. This was the early 90's. We didn't even have MapQuest yet, let alone a cell phone or google. Someone hand wrote the directions for me. Another cowboy gingerly helped Steve into the passenger's seat and wished me luck as he shut the door.

I got the truck started and then we did the herky-jerky out of the parking lot. Even in his injured state, he somehow had the patience to coach me a little on how to smoothly switch gears. We arrived at the ER after about a twenty minute drive, got him stitched up and then headed back to the Springs. He drove.

Steve's First Sergeant wasn't really happy with him come Monday. I think the exact quote, minus military language was, "Sgt. R, I don't care what you do on the weekends, but you better be ready to work and in deployable shape on Mondays. This better not happen again."

Of course, this butt chewing didn't stop him from riding, but he was a bit more careful to turn out a bull that was above his skill level.

Cowboy Courtship

Easter came around a few weeks after we met. I convinced him to go to church with me. We attended the Methodist church that met in the little White Chapel on Flying W Ranch in Colorado Springs. He liked it and that became our church home. Steve was a little uncomfortable that first Sunday as people kept staring at him. He was one week out from the Captain Marvel run in and still looked pretty rough. After church, we drove up Rampart Range road, a dirt road that rises out of Garden of the Gods which is a city-owned park that is full of stunning red rock formations. It's a must on any tourist to do list when they visit Colorado Springs.

The views up Rampart Range Road of the Rockies and the valleys below are breathtaking any time of year. On this spring day, the Colorado blue sky was cloudless. Evidence of new life and the promise of new beginnings was all around us. The pasqueflowers had on their royal purple in on honor of Easter and spring. The magnificent aspen trees and oaks were showing small leaf buds. The possibility of new love made my heart soar. We stopped at an overlook, stepped out of the truck, and just quietly enjoyed the beauty that surrounded us for few minutes. One of us thought to bring a camera. We took pictures of each other at the overlook to commemorate Easter Sunday and what it means. The day was special. The place was special. This moment in time was special.

Ring shopping began over the summer. He called my Dad to ask his permission to marry me while I was out of town on business. The Saturday after I got home, we went to a cowboy poetry gathering, grabbed some lunch at Taco Bell, his favorite fast food restaurant, and then took a drive back up Rampart Range Road. I had a sneaking suspicion something was up and thought, *"This is it!"* I was right. He parked at the lookout where we'd stopped on Easter Sunday, all of four months ago. He took my hand, led me to a giant boulder and asked me to sit down. With great chivalry, he went down on one knee, pulled a small box out of his jacket pocket, opened it up to expose the ring and said, "I love you. It would thrill me to death if you would be my wife."

I responded through happy tears, "There is nothing I want more, and I can't wait to be your wife!"

The next thing Steve said was something I held dear to my heart for a very long time. "I chose this mountain to propose to you, because like our love, it will always be here," he said as he pulled me close for a kiss.

"I love you," I said.

"I love you more," he replied.

The romantic gesture of proposing at this scenic place was typical of Steve. He regularly wrote me poems and gave me beautiful cards with heartfelt messages, to which he always added his own. He wrote this poem placed in my Christmas card the year we got engaged.

Let Me Walk This Angel Home
Yes sir, it's me again.
I'm not calling to complain.
If you've got a minute, I've got something to ask of you
It won't take long, just a few
I don't quite know when it happened,
but I think I've found something that might belong to you.
You see sir, I've heard you're the Giving Kind
And well, I was just wondering if you would mind…
Let me walk this Angel home.
Let me hold her close to me.
Let me feel the love she gives so free.
If you'll just let her stay, no harm, I promise will come her way.
Lord, just let me walk this Angel home.

You know sir, I've been working on my mouth
and I've sworn off that drinkin'
Heck, I can't even remember the last time I was honky-tonkin'.
I've been to church a couple times, this month,
I think it's been three.
Sir, that preacher says there's hope for even me.

I know she's from up above
'cause she gives me the kind of love the Bible talks of.

So, sir, if it don't put you in a bind
And if you don't really mind.
Let me walk this Angel home.
Let me hold her close to me.
Let me feel the love she gives so free.
If you'll just let her stay, no harm, I promise will come her way.
Lord, just let me walk this Angel home.

When I read these words that Christmas morning, I was overcome with emotion. I felt safe, secure, and completely loved. These beautiful words were coming from the man who would be my husband. What woman wouldn't love a guy who said and wrote these kinds of things to her? I took this as a commitment on his part for our upcoming nuptials. For me, this was the cowboy way of saying until 'death do us part.' He often called me his angel and we both referred back to this poem and the meaning behind it in cards and letters we shared through our engagement and marriage.

Western Wedding

We set the wedding date for February 20th, almost exactly a year from the day we met. That gave me six months to plan a wedding. Since my job at JA was essentially special event planning, I figured I could put a wedding together in six months' time. It was to be held in Hot Springs, South Dakota in the church where I was raised.

February is right smack dab in the middle of calving season for my family. This date selection was not a popular choice. It was an evening wedding. It was cold that night. So cold. You could see your breath cold. Single-digit cold. Skip, the pastor from our church in Colorado Springs did the honors. It was a western themed wedding, complete with wagon wheel décor and antique oil lamps in the church windows. We took pictures after the ceremony and as the wedding party and family completed their picture taking responsibilities they each departed to the reception.

The reception was about a football field length away, at the other end of the parking lot. We got down to the ringbearer, flower girl, matron of honor, the best man and of course the bride and groom. It was then we realized the only person with a vehicle was the groom. I forgot to make transportation arrangements to get us to the reception. Steve took the kids first, then the matron of honor and best man.

For a moment, I was alone in the church. My heart was full of gratitude for what a wonderful day it had been. I thought my heart would burst from sheer joy. I'd just married the kindest man I knew besides my dad and my brothers. The future was a blank slate and I was so excited to build a life with my quiet, thoughtful cowboy.

Country Living

We honeymooned in Vegas. Once back in Colorado Springs, he cleared out of the military. This is a 30-day process that a soldier goes through at the end of their enlistment. He got the process done in two weeks. That chapter of his life was done. He found a job rather quickly. We also realized our little one-bedroom apartment wasn't large enough. We had a lot of wedding gifts and nowhere to put them! Luckily, our lease was up so we were able to move. He found a little rental house for us. It was a six-month lease. This was good as he found a better job a few months later that provided a home for us on the property, so we moved again in July.

The new job was a caretaker for a little 300-acre place just south of Colorado Springs. It was country living and this country girl was tickled pink! The JA headquarters was about a 15-minute drive to the north, so was convenient for me. He was responsible for fixing the fence, clearing the road when it snowed, feeding, and mucking the stalls of two horses, feeding two old broken down dairy cows as well as two obnoxious donkeys. Since the job required we live there, they paid all our utilities except long distance phone calls. There was no washer and dryer hookup, so I did laundry up the road at the owners home. Steve hauled water once a week to keep our cistern full. The well had gone dry years before. These minor inconveniences didn't bother me. Living out of town on 300 acres more than made up for it.

Over Thanksgiving that year, Steve went to a Lyle Sankey rodeo school. Lyle Sankey is a very accomplished all-around rough stock rider and a strong Christian man. His schools are about learning to ride better, but he always shares the gospel. Steve accepted Christ at this school. So that right there will tell you how green I was in my faith. I had no idea the man I was married to wasn't even saved! I never asked.

Steve's parents were divorced, but they were both believers and had strong faith. His dad attended a mega church in California and his mom attended church in Boise, Idaho. Since I knew he was raised to believe in God, I just assumed he was a believer.

As a new believer, Steve became hungry for God's Word. I too wanted to understand God. I genuinely wanted to learn how to be a godly wife. We began individual Bible study. We talked about what we were learning. I was so proud of who we were as a couple. I loved where we lived. I loved who we were becoming.

Steve and I, along with another couple re-started a chapter of the Fellowship of Christian Cowboys in the Colorado Springs area. We were part of a small group Bible study through our church. We attended church every week. We went to Sunday school. We tithed. We prayed together. I had a good job. He was going to school and wanted to become a vet. We dreamed together about our future. We had so many plans. We had all the newly married and Christian boxes checked. Life was perfect. I was so confident in us.

Then one warm spring night Steve didn't come home from his night class until the wee hours of the morning. Of course, I was waiting up, worried sick. He parked his truck and staggered into the barn. I followed him. He was stinking drunk and was determined to sleep in the hay. I learned you can't reason with a drunk. I went to bed, relieved he was home, but devastated that he was drinking after being sober for over two years.

This moral failure put a lot of strain on our new marriage. We celebrated our one-year anniversary just a couple months before. A few days later, I had to go out of town on business. I fought the urge to call Steve and see if he was home each night. I knew the answer in my heart. I found out years later I was right. He wasn't home.

I came home to a broken, repentant man. He found a Christian based 12-step program and began to attend. He remained distant from me for several weeks. I wanted to talk. I wanted to understand why. But above all, I wanted 'it' to be fixed and for us to get back to who we were before. In retrospect, I handled it all wrong. I poked. I prodded. I pushed. The more I did these things, the more he pulled away. The strain between us was fierce. It was clear he was really struggling with something. I had no idea at the time with what and he wasn't in a mood to share.

I came home from work one afternoon to find him sitting on the porch steps of our little house. He was wearing a ball cap and a t-shirt, tucked into his size 28 waist Wranglers. He had a cup of coffee in his hand and a cup of hot tea prepared for me. For the first time in weeks, he smiled at me and welcomed me home. Clearly something had changed in him. He signaled for me to take a seat next to him. I complied.

"I can't tell you enough how sorry I am for putting you through this," he began. "I can't promise it will never happen again, but I'm going to do my very best to stay sober. You deserve that. I know it scared you."

"Yes," I replied, "it terrified me. What if that was how our life was every day? I don't think I could take that."

"You shouldn't have to," he said matter-of-factly.

He took my hand in his, looked at me with those sad and serious blue eyes and said, "I love you."

"I love you more," I responded.

"Now, I have something else I want to talk to you about," he said with a firmness in his voice. "I've decided I miss the Army and I want to go back in. I think the discipline of the Army is just what I need right now."

My world tumbled down around me. If the drinking had scared me, the shock of this announcement literally tore my heart out. I was terrified. I had no idea how it all worked. The year we dated, I didn't pay attention. He was getting out after all. I was NOT going to be a military spouse. I knew nothing. I didn't understand the language. I didn't understand ranks. I am quite sure I didn't understand the difference between, enlisted and officers. For at least a week, I begged. I pleaded. I negotiated with him to stay the course with college and to keep our nice little life the way it was. He was not having it. He was going back in and we were moving on.

The next week he drove to the Denver Military Entrance Processing Station (MEPS) to re-enlist. I was hoping he would call me at work with news of his assignment before I had to leave for a dentist appointment. Just as I was getting ready to head out, the phone rang at my desk.

"This is Audrey," I said as I answered.

"Hi Angel," he said, "I hoped I'd catch you before you left for your appointment."

"I was just getting ready to go," I replied. "What did you find out? Is it Texas?"

"Nope," he said, "It's way better. I've been assigned to the 82nd Airborne!"

"Where is that?" I asked with dread.

"Ft. Bragg, North Carolina! I'm going to be Airborne and assigned to one of the best units in the Army!" he said with awe and excitement.

"That's great Steve," I replied, trying my best to muster up some type of sincerity. "I'll see you at home. I have to go or I'm going to be late."

I put the phone back in its cradle. North Carolina. Ugh. Up to this point in my life, I had lived in four states; South Dakota, Nebraska, Iowa, and Colorado. These states touch each other. I'm a Midwestern girl through and through. My people say things like, it's *busted*, instead of broken. We say *pop* instead of soda or coke. We wave at each other on the highway even when we don't know each other. I spent a lot of time in the South growing up visiting my mother's family in Alabama. I hate the humidity of the South. I hate the bugs of the South. The people are great, but the weather leaves a lot to be desired. North Carolina could have been Siberia. It felt so far away and so foreign. I didn't want to go. I didn't want to be an Army wife. But, as a Christian wife, I must go where my husband went. We were moving to North Carolina.

When one has a dentist appointment that is a couple-hour procedure, one has a long time to think. As I lay back in the chair with the extremely attractive rubber dam fully in place, the reality of how my life was about to change slowly sank in. I couldn't stop the tears from leaking out of both eyes and rolling down into my ears.

Becoming an Army Wife

It took us a few months to get there. Since he was assigned a different job in the Army than before, he was required to go through several weeks of training at Ft. Benning, Georgia. This created a problem. We couldn't get our orders to move until he had an official duty station. It would be at least three months before this would happen. We lived where he worked. I dreaded the thought of moving twice, so I came up with a solution. I would quit my job and do his for the summer. I looked at his job description, came up with a schedule and took my idea to the boss lady. I identified two things on the list I didn't feel I was physically able to accomplish; fix fence and drive the road grader.

She thought about it overnight and called me the next day to say, "We have a deal."

Other than missing him terribly, I thoroughly enjoyed that summer. Being outside so much really suited me. I had a great deal of time to study God's Word, exercise, and read. I could have stayed there forever, but the day came that we had orders. My first official interaction with the Army as an Army wife was to go on Ft. Carson and make the arrangements for the move to Ft. Bragg. We knew he was going to Airborne school, also at Ft. Benning, after he was done with Advanced Individual Training (AIT). That was a three-week school. Since I had several weeks to kill, I drove to South Dakota and spent a few days with my parents. Then, I drove to Alabama.

My mother's family all live near Birmingham, Alabama. My Uncle Gene had a cabin outside of town. He was spending his summer there and invited me to come stay with him. Normally, I would have stayed with my Grandmother, but I had my dog, OD, with me and she wasn't allowed pets at her little apartment. Uncle Gene's cabin became my headquarters until Steve was done with school.

It was a two-hour drive to Ft. Benning, Georgia from my uncle's cabin. I was able to see Steve graduate from AIT. He was free on the weekends after that, so I would go pick him up on Fridays. We'd spend the weekend at the cabin with Uncle Gene and then it was back to Ft. Benning on Sundays. Finally, after three weeks of this, Airborne School was done, and we were heading to North Carolina. We pulled out on a Friday evening and drove the eight hours to Fayetteville. We found a pet friendly hotel and fell into bed.

Saturday morning came with new responsibilities. My job was to find us a place to live. His first order of business was to check in to the unit. During AIT, he learned of a special unit, Long Range Surveillance Company (LRSC), and he worked to get his orders changed from the 82nd to the LRSC. He was successful. Not only did one have to have an airborne tab to serve in this unit, one had to have a Ranger Tab. Ranger school would be in his future. The job of LRSC operators is surveillance, reconnaissance, and target acquisitions. Most of this is done behind enemy lines in a conflict. This company was brand new and not fully staffed yet. The company commander reported directly to the Installation Commander, General Hugh Shelton. This unit was pretty high speed and dangerous. It was also a great opportunity for him and everything he had ever wanted to do in the Army.

As for me, I was going along to get along. I still didn't want to be there. I still didn't want to be a military wife. Yet here I was. I couldn't find a job in my field. This was a problem I'd never faced before. My background was non-profit work. It's expensive to train a new person and the likelihood I would leave in three years was high. Not to be deterred, I jumped in with both feet to life as an Army wife. The second week we were there, I took a class for new military spouses to learn how the Army worked. I also signed up for Army Family Team Building. (AFTB) Not only did I take all the classes that I was allowed per my tenure as a military spouse, I became an instructor and taught every module to Family Support Groups all around Ft. Bragg during my time there. I joined Protestant Women of the Chapel (PWOC) and volunteered at the Army Community Service (ACS) office.

PWOC was a Godsend. I made lifelong friends there. These women helped me gain perspective in my pity party. Even though I was doing all these activities and getting involved, I was still feeling sorry for myself. Our income had been cut almost in half and we had added bills. Where we didn't have to pay rent and utilities prior, now we did. Instead of living out in the countryside of Colorado, we were living in a run-down, two-bedroom trailer house outside of Fayetteville. At least it was in the country.

Even though I struggled to find work, we could make it on his income as we had no debt other than my school loan and one car payment. I managed our money and I figured out how to make it work. I can stretch a dollar, but I resented having to make all these adjustments.

And I was scared. What if he drank again? We were far away from family. What if he had to go to war? What if he died? What if I embarrassed him in some way because I didn't know the rules of rank or the military way, or worse, got him into trouble because of my ignorance? Our life was perfectly fine in Colorado. I was happy there. I was very unhappy with all the change. And, I was totally convinced that no one had ever been this miserable or hurt as a military spouse.

I shared my pitiful selfish attitude with my small group at PWOC. We'd been there about one month. It was probably my third time with the group. There were two women in the group that day that were a few years older than I.

Marilyn, who became a very dear friend, looked me in the eye and asked with gentleness and wisdom, "Have you told Steve how you feel?"

"Well no," I responded.

Marilyn continued to look at me with a steady gaze and said, "You should start there. He needs to know how you're feeling. Secondly, while you might believe that this is awfully hard, and I'm not saying it isn't, almost every woman around this table has had a difficult experience being an Army wife. Perhaps

Janie's story will help give you a little perspective. Jane, would you mind sharing?"

With a pained look on her face and in her eyes, Janie shared with me how her husband had been killed in a helicopter crash during Desert Storm. She explained how difficult that was to cope with, then and now. Another woman told me she had three small children at home and how hard it was every time her husband had to go to a school or down range for training. She basically was a single mom for months out of the year. Someone else shared that she had difficult health issues that she had to cope with while her husband was gone. She too had children.

One by one these women helped me realize that all I was really dealing with was change. It was okay that I didn't like it. They helped me realize how prideful I was being, thinking that no one could possibly understand what a sacrifice I had made. Compared to Janie, I had made no sacrifice whatsoever. I left that Bible study appropriately spanked by wise and wonderful women of God. I got in my truck and just sat for a moment, reflecting on what just happened. Then I started laughing. I laughed at myself and my selfish stupidity. I thanked God for showing me truth. I thanked God for showing me that, like in farming and ranching, the military is the family business. I was going to get on board and be an excellent Army wife.

That night over supper, I came clean with Steve and also shared what I'd learned that day. I gave him my word I was all in.

Chapter 3
The Wheels Came Off

"I'm chewin', drinkin' and cheatin' on my wife."

Life at Ft. Bragg

We settled into life at Ft. Bragg. We got on-post housing after a year. He was gone long periods of time for training. He got his Ranger tab, graduated HALO (High Altitude Low Open) parachute school and completed SERE (Survival, Evasion, Resistance, and Escape) School, which is a school to learn how to survive as a POW. When he was home, we were happy. We had a nice routine and an easy steady way of being together. I would even say there was a sweetness between us as we grew as a couple and spiritually.

We had a routine I treasured. Saturday mornings we slept in. The first one up made the coffee. We sat in bed for a couple of hours talking and drinking coffee. We talked about everything; what God was teaching us in our individual walk, how work was going for him and the details of his last school or training, our future, our past, the volunteer work I was doing and later, the part-time work I had. We'd fix a late breakfast together and then do whatever tasks needed to be done that day. Sundays were of course church in the morning and then a long afternoon nap. On the weekdays we would rise early. We only had one car, so I would drop him at the unit and then go work out. I was done with my physical training (PT) every day before the Army was! After the evening meal, he would make a cup of tea for me and, coffee for himself. We would talk over the day. He helped me cook and do the dishes. We didn't watch much TV; we just enjoyed each other's company.

I struggled to find work in my field as a non-profit professional. Just sitting around the house was not an option; I needed something to do to fill the long months he was gone, so I started my own training business and landed a steady gig with the local community college. I taught personal development to middle level managers at several factories around town for the college. My money was what we had fun with, bought extra things needed for the house or put into savings. I was on the board for PWOC and led a small group Bible study for them. I developed sweet friendships with women and remained active in AFTB. This program was designed after the Gulf War to prepare Army spouses for deployment. AFTB is a fabulous program that did a lot to teach me about how the military worked. I was so involved, that I got picked by the Department of Defense to spend a week in Washington, DC with other spouses to help re-write the curriculum. Such an honor! For someone who was a reluctant military spouse, I found my stride and a way to thrive!

We had a home church and were in a couples Bible study run by the Navigators. My friend Marilyn and her husband Dave led that study. Steve was very faithful to have an early morning quiet time with the Lord, as was I. He also started a Bible study with his unit.

Despite all of this, I had a constant nagging worry in the back of my mind. What if he drank again? Every time he left for a school I worried. I prayed, but I worried. I didn't trust sobriety. Truthfully, I didn't trust Steve to stay sober. I was especially bothered by the fact that he refused to attend AA or a faith-based recovery program.

Late one night, after we had been at Ft. Bragg for a couple of years, I got a collect call from him while he was at HALO school in California. He was drunk. Crying. Apologizing. I finally got him off the phone. There was nothing I could do to help him or encourage him in that state. It had happened again. My worst fears realized. We talked the next day. He was broken and determined to do better. Upon his return home, it was as if it never happened. As I recall, we had one brief conversation about it. He didn't want to talk about it much. So, the episode essentially got swept under the rug. We just went back to our routine. He was sober and that was all that really mattered to me.

As our time at Ft. Bragg was winding down, Steve began meeting regularly with a Chaplain friend of his. Steve decided not to re-enlist. Instead, he was going to get out of the Army and move us to Portland, Oregon so he could attend Mult-nomah College of the Bible. He wanted to go to seminary. This Chaplain was mentoring and discipling Steve and was instrumental in helping him decide where to go to seminary.

Steve was taking classes at a local Bible college. One of his favorite instructors was in the process of planting a church in Fayetteville. Steve and I both enjoyed his teaching, so we started attending that church in January of 1997, just a few months before he was to separate from the Army. One spring Sunday in late April, the guest pastor didn't show up. A leader in the church asked Steve to give his testimony. It was a powerful one. He had less than five minutes to prepare, so there's no doubt in my mind God gave him the words and the message to deliver that morning. There wasn't a dry eye in the place.

Make no mistake, satan saw that and said, "Nope. Can't have that. Can't have this young man head off to Bible College. He'll be too powerful in the Lord. We better put a stop to it."

And he did. He knew just how to get to Steve. The bottle.

Satan's Trap

Steve's brother, Rob, was getting married in Idaho in May. To better prepare for our big move, we decided Steve would fly to Boise, Idaho to see his mom, go to the wedding, and then take a few days to drive to Oregon and visit the college. We thought this would be a helpful step to get the lay of the land for scholarships, housing, and even jobs for both of us. This was the late 90's. The Internet was barely a thing. So, researching these sorts of things on-line was a non-existent option.

The next week after his testimony, I could tell something was wrong. He seemed angry and distant. There were other signs that something was up with him. He was later than usual getting home from work one day and I thought I smelled beer on his breath. He denied it. I pressed him a couple more times about his changes in behavior. He acknowledged he was struggling with something, but he told me he had to work it out on his own. He didn't want to talk about it. I asked him point blank if he was struggling to stay sober. He denied that. Finally, I let it go. After all, he was getting ready to move us across the country, leaving behind health insurance, a steady paycheck, and all that was familiar to go to seminary. We were planning to make yet another change based on what he wanted. I concluded he might be having doubts and was perhaps a little stressed about it. This seemed natural and normal. So, I left it alone.

I put him on a plane May 1st at the Raleigh airport. He called me when he got to his mother's. He called again when he got to Rob's for the wedding two days later. I was working a part-time, temporary job with Youth for Christ in Fayetteville. The executive director invited me to go to a conference in Asheville with the whole staff during the time Steve was gone. The plan was for me to drive our car to Raleigh and park it at the airport. I would ride on to Asheville with my co-workers. Steve's return ticket was for the same day the conference started. The car would be there for him in Raleigh to drive back to Fayetteville.

There was something so off in his behavior prior to his departure and something off in that second phone call that I became concerned. I spent the next two days praying and fasting, asking the Lord for guidance. He told me very clearly to stay home and not go to the conference. I didn't understand why, but I knew I needed to be obedient. I went to my boss and explained what the Lord was telling me. He agreed to let me out of the conference.

The next step was to get word to Steve that I would be picking him up and the car wouldn't be at the airport after all. He was supposed to go back to Boise that night and stay with his mother, flying out the next morning. I called her and asked her to have Steve call me when he got in. That call never came. I laid awake all-night waiting. My phone rang at 6 a.m. It was my mother-in-law, not Steve. She, too, had been up all night. She confirmed what I suspected. He hadn't come in and she was hoping he'd called me. Both of us were concerned. We also both acknowledged it was likely he was drinking, but where? Or was he dead in a ditch somewhere?

She decided to drive to the Boise airport and see if he arrived there. She didn't see him, but when she asked the desk clerk if he had checked in, they said he was listed on the manifest. Not exactly a yes, but she thought I should drive to the airport in Raleigh just in case. In the meantime, she went to the rental car place. When I called her to tell her he wasn't on the plane, she told me he hadn't turned in the rental car, but got the manager to agree to call her when it was turned in.

Where in the world was Steve, and how was I going to search for him when he was presumably on the West coast and I was on the East coast? The first thing I did was call family and close friends to let them know Steve was missing. I needed to get the prayer warriors up and running! I also called one of my Youth for Christ co-workers so they could be praying as well.

Next, I called his brother Rob. No, he hadn't seen Steve since the wedding. No, he hadn't heard from him either. As far as Rob knew, he'd gone to Portland. Strike one. I called the college. Yes, Steve had come to his first meeting to talk about financial aid, but he seemed distracted. He didn't keep his follow up appointment. Strike two. I called all the Fellowship of Christian Cowboy chapters in Oregon and Idaho to see if Steve had been to one of their meetings or been in touch with them, as this was something he'd mentioned he might do. Nope. Strike three. I called the Chaplain Steve had been meeting with to get his brother's phone number. The Chaplains brother lived in Portland and Steve had planned to stay with him while he was there. Called the brother. Nope. He hadn't heard from Steve either. Struck out again.

Remember that part where I was worried I would do something to embarrass my husband or hurt his career? Yeah, so calling the Army officer, who was also a friend and Chaplain, triggered a call from my husband's unit. The phone rang.

"Hello," I answered.

"Mrs. R?" the caller queried.

"Speaking," I said.

"This is the First Sergeant. I just had a call from the Company Commander. I understand your husband is missing. Can you tell me what's going on?"

Well, I didn't really KNOW anything, except he hadn't gotten on the plane he was supposed to be on, and he wasn't following through on his plans for his time in Portland. So, I protected his reputation. I didn't share what I actually thought was happening. I just said he missed his plane.

"I'm sure the reason he hasn't called to tell me he had a change of plans is he thinks I'm not home. I'm supposed to be at a conference in Asheville," I explained. I didn't add he didn't have the courtesy to call his mother and she was worried sick.

"Well," said the First Sergeant with great skepticism in his voice, "if you hear from him, you make sure to remind him that his leave is up at midnight on May 9th. If he's not back, he will be AWOL (Absent Without Leave). I hope everything turns out okay ma'am."

"Thank you for your call First Sergeant. I'm sure everything will be fine," I said with as much conviction I could muster up.

I understood why the good Chaplain felt compelled to inform Steve's chain of command he might be missing. As Steve said later when he learned of this, "You didn't call the Chaplain. You called the United States Army!"

The unit was onto him and the fact that he wasn't where his wife expected him to be.

I resumed my search. His mother called again with phone numbers to the State Patrol in Oregon and Idaho. She strongly suggested I call and put an APB out on him. She gave me the details of the rental car. Agreeing this was a prudent course of action, I did just that. While on the phone with the female patrol officer from Idaho, she asked, "Did you say your husband is in the Army?"

"Yes ma'am," I answered.

"Is he on leave?" she asked.

"Yes ma'am," I responded.

"You know, the Army owns his butt. If he's not back by the time his leave is up, he will be AWOL and the Army will go hunting for him. Until then, you might as well relax. There's not much you can do. Let the Army handle this," she advised.

I knew he would be AWOL if he didn't make it back by midnight May 9th. I hadn't thought about the fact the Army would look for him. This gave me hope. It then dawned on me that he would need money if he was staying in Portland. I called the bank and sure enough, withdrawals were being made in Portland. I determined then he'd either been held at gunpoint and given up the pin number for the card or he was binge drinking in Portland. The second was the more likely scenario and meant he was likely alive! This was May 6th.

It was a long four days until the 9th. I checked the bank account daily. He was getting daily withdrawals and always at the same ATM. It would be pretty easy for the Army to find him. I would provide them with the ATM information. That is if he didn't come home. I concluded that even drunk, he was still a good soldier. He would not become AWOL.

The morning of the 9th, his mother called me. The rental car was dropped off. It had damage to the front end. Nice. I checked our credit card. An airline ticket was purchased that morning at the Boise airport. Upon a little further detective work, I determined when he would likely make a connection in the Chicago airport and what time he would arrive in Raleigh. I paged him in Chicago. Relief washed over me in waves when I heard his voice. Of course, he was quite confused. I was supposed to be in Asheville at the conference. Why was I calling him in Chicago and how did I know he was there? The conversation was cool and brief. This concerned me, but I wasn't too worried about it. I didn't know exactly what he'd been up to, but now he knew I knew things weren't right. I was just relieved he was located and coming home!

For the third time in nine days, I made the trip to the Raleigh airport. This time, to my relief, he got off the plane. He was home. I had so many questions. I wanted to know where he'd been and what had happened to him. What I learned would break my heart. He told me that he had cheated on me multiple times in our marriage. The first was when we were still in Colorado Springs while I was away on business. There were two other times. The second time was at HALO school. The third he was away on training with his unit. Each time alcohol was a factor. I wasn't surprised about the drinking. The cheating shocked me!

He told me he'd met someone in Portland. This time it was different. It wasn't just a drunken one-night stand. He'd spent four *whole* days with her. He met her at a bar. She was his bartender. Her name was Jennifer.

"I'm in love with her. I'm leaving you for her. I'm through," he told me with great anger in his voice, as we drove toward Ft.

Bragg in the darkness of a cloud covered North Carolina summer night.

I was confused by his anger. The rage in his tone didn't line up with his words.

"What about Bible College?" I asked, confused, trying to keep up with how rapidly my life was unravelling.

"I'm chewin', drinkin' and cheatin' on my wife. I don't think I'm in any spiritual condition to go to Bible College, do you?" he retorted.

I sat in stunned silence for quite a bit. I was trying to process everything he'd just thrown at me. He'd cheated. More than once. He considered himself to be in love with his barkeep. *Whatever.* He was going to Portland without me. I started asking questions, but he sat in stone cold silence the rest of the drive.

When we got home, he threw some things into a duffel bag. He planned to sleep at the unit for the night. Plus, he had to check back in from leave. With twenty minutes to spare, he backed out of the parking space to go check in. The relief of having found him and having him back alive was completely overridden with a new pain. The pain of grief set in. My marriage of four short years was likely over, seemingly derailed by four short days with some woman named Jennifer. The man I loved so much and had sacrificed so much for believed himself to be in love with another woman. I watched him pull away, then walked slowly back into the house and collapsed on the couch in tears. I didn't just cry. I sobbed. I sobbed like a two-year-old sobs; guttural, loud and in wails.

Chapter 4
You've Got a Friend

**"I looked at myself in the mirror the other day and
asked myself what happened?"**

Comfort In A Crisis

It would have been prudent to just go to bed. It was after 1
a.m. before I got the sobbing under control. The emotional
pain of rejection from your beloved is acute. We're meant to
cleave, not to leave. I realized I was distraught and in crisis. I'm
a calm, steady person by nature. Also, a control enthusiast and
the one who typically takes charge of a situation help others.
This feeling of being completely out of control with seemingly
no ability to influence the outcome of the new situation I found
myself in was unfamiliar territory.

I called my friend Marilyn. A true friend, the person who
really loves you, will pull herself out of bed at 1 a.m. and come
to your home. She will sit with you. She will listen. She will cry
with you. She will pray with you and she will give you sage,

godly advice. My friend Marilyn is that kind of friend. She stayed until well after 2 a.m. After I caught her up on what transpired, she looked at me and said the words I didn't want to hear but needed to be said, "Audrey, there's no guarantee how this will turn out."

What I wanted to hear was everything was going to be okay. I wanted assurance that Steve would pull his head out of his fourth point of contact and get over this silly idea he was in love with a woman he barely knew. I wanted to be told my marriage was not over. That's what I wanted to hear. What I needed to hear was truth. There *was* no guarantee. Marilyn spoke truth into my life at the moment I needed it most.

Then she said, "Through this you're first going to learn that God is sufficient. Then you're going to learn that God *alone* is sufficient." How prophetic those words proved to be.

Before she left, she prayed. When she prayed over me she asked God to give me the strength I needed to get through this crisis and that I would get through it with dignity. After she prayed, she looked me in the eye and said, "Be careful to conduct yourself through this in a manner that you will have no regrets. Be mindful of the decisions you make and in your interaction with Steve".

I'm so grateful my friends spoke truth into my life during this time. Another older sister in Christ taught me that God is a God of economy; He doesn't waste experiences. In the spirit of this truth, Marilyn, while comforting me, was teaching me how to comfort others when the time came. This concept is taken from 2 Corinthians 1:3-4

"Blessed be the God and Father of our Lord Jesus Christ, the Father of mercies and God of all comfort; who

comforts us in all our affliction so that we may be able to
comfort those who are in any affliction with the comfort
with which we ourselves are comforted by God."

Marilyn did several things that are great examples of what
comfort looks like. She was physically present. She was also
truthful. It would have been so easy to throw platitudes and
insincere promises at the situation. Speaking the truth in love
is hard to do. It's also hard to hear, but it's the correct thing in
crisis or grief. She encouraged me by speaking spiritual truths
into my heart. She prayed over me. Lastly, she admonished me
to conduct myself and behave in a godly manner as I walked
through whatever came next. Such an excellent example and a
model I have often followed when comforting others.

There were three couples in our life that poured themselves
into us and into the situation; Marilyn and her husband Dave,
who were in full time ministry and led our couples Bible Study;
Pam and Vern, and Gina and Jason. Vern and Jason were in
Steve's unit. All six of us attended the same church. Gina and
Jason were also in our couples Bible Study. These people were
our Army family.

I first met Pam at a Family Readiness Group (FRG) meeting.
Her husband Vern was the platoon sergeant, so that meant she
had the job of looking out for all of us wives. I knew the very
moment I heard her speak that she loved Jesus. Jesus practically
oozed out of her pores. When I got home and told Steve that I
thought Sgt and Mrs. Tubbs were Christians he responded that
he doubted it. I guess Vern was tough on the guys at work. The
very next Sunday, we were sitting in an adult Sunday school
class in the front row. The teacher posed a question and Vern

sounded off the answer from the back row. We didn't know he
and Pam were in the room. Steve came to seated attention.

"What are you doing?" I whispered.

"That's Sgt Tubbs," he whispered back.

"We're in church, I doubt he expects you to be at attention," I
gently answered trying not to laugh.

It was clear Steve had mad respect for the man. Over time, we
became good friends. We had dinner in one another's homes
often and Pam and I got together for tea, lunch, or coffee almost
regularly.

We met Gina and Jason some time later. Jason was the 'new
guy' in the unit and Steve invited them to church. I think I
scared Gina to death as I immediately invited her to PWOC,
our couples study and to lunch. She's a much more reserved
person than I. My attempt to be welcoming was a bit over the
top, I'll admit. Despite my awkward attempts at welcoming her,
we became good friends. She told me later she wasn't sure how
to react to such gushing excitement. They soon became members of our couples study and she did become a highly active
member of PWOC. We were there for each other through the
ups and downs of army life.

Marilyn, Pam and Gina gave me the gift of listening. How
weary they must have grown hearing me say the same things
over and over as I processed my new reality. Daily there were
new developments in my drama. They listened to that too.
These women cried with me. It felt so good to cry with women.
I felt loved and cherished. It seemed to me that God's tears min-
gled with mine as his servants cried with me. Their hugs were
hugs from Him.

These friends included me in their daily activities to make
sure I wasn't alone all of the time. The couples rotated me

through their homes almost nightly for the evening meal throughout the first month. Marilyn took me shoe shopping one day and had me ride with her another day to go get a friend at the airport. Pam took me golfing. Gina and Jason, who had both been through a divorce, gave excellent financial advice and support. I was at their house most often.

The men got involved with Steve. Vern spent a couple of hours with Steve the day after he got back from Portland. Vern later shared it was a difficult conversation. He kept the details between him and Steve, as a true friend does.

Jason called me the evening after Steve returned. He and Gina were checking in on me and wondered how our reunion had gone. I filled him in, including the part about the other woman and that he was leaving me for her. Jason told me he would talk to him the next morning at work. The following evening Jason called me to tell me that he walked into the arms room where Steve worked and all he could think to say was, "How was your trip?"

Jason got a short, two-word reply that I can't put in a Christian book. Needless to say, it wasn't a fruitful conversation.

Church Discipline

Besides being lovingly truthful, our friends were present in our lives. They were in constant prayer for both of us. Not only did our male friends get involved with Steve, so did leaders from our church. The Chaplain who had been mentoring Steve talked with him on more than one occasion. We were members of a wonderful non-denominational church that preached the Bible. The good Chaplain took the situation to our church leadership. There were four men who prayerfully decided to take

Steve through the steps of church discipline. Matthew 18:15-17 says:

> *"If your brother sins go and show him his fault in*
> *private; if he listens to you, you have won your brother.*
> *But if he does not listen to you, take one or two more with*
> *you, so that by the mouth of two or three witnesses every*
> *fact may be confirmed. If he refuses to listen to them tell*
> *it to the church; and if he refuses to listen even to the*
> *church, let him be to you as a Gentile and a tax collector."*

Vern was one of those men. He visited with Steve alone at least once. The Chaplain, who also attended our church, and was the Chaplain assigned to Steve's unit, spoke with him more than once. This is step one in the process.

Two weeks after his return, Pam, Vern, and the Chaplain came to my house. We were all fasting. We prayed together. The men left to go find Steve. We were at step two in the church accountability process. Pam and I stayed and continued to pray over the meeting. The men found Steve and talked to him, but returned and reported no change in the situation.

A few days later, two pastors from our church and the Chaplain found Steve at the barracks. This satisfied the third step in the accountability process. One of the pastors called me after to tell me what had transpired in the conversation.

"He's very resolved in this course of action, but at the same time, he is in great turmoil and is unable to resolve things in his mind. He's unable to make peace with God," said the pastor. A few days later, the senior pastor delivered a letter from our church to Steve removing him from membership.

Answered Prayer

The morning of June 1st began like every other day since May 10th. My pain nudged me awake like an old friend. A full month had passed since first putting Steve on that plane. We'd started a conversation about a separation agreement. Our church family and our friends had done all they could. Many were still praying for a miracle. I was beginning to understand things could never go back to 'normal'. So much damage had been done to our marriage. I also was realizing the odds of reconciliation were not good. I held out hope anyway. The hope of reconciliation juxtaposed against reality caused me to have super raw emotions. Limbo is a tough place to be.

Then the phone rang. It was Steve.

"I want to come back home if you'll let me. I broke up with Jennifer," he said.

He went on to say that we would need individual counseling and counseling together. He also said that he had learned he did love me.

I was floored. I was ecstatic! Maybe, I was a bit too eager. This was what I had prayed for. This was what many had prayed for! Wasn't this God answering our prayers?! Of course, I said yes, and that afternoon he was home.

When I asked him what changed he said, "The forty-eight hours after the letter from the church was delivered, the world got really dark. I stayed sober for those two days and could really hear God."

As is the case in many things of God, there is an underlying spiritual mystery that can't be explained in our earthly reality. When believers obey God and do the sometimes-difficult things he asks of us as instructed in scripture, he works in and through those acts of obedience. Steve responded to the church discipline and it was clear that God was at work in Steve's brokenness.

As we talked, God brought to my mind a memory that occurred in late April. Someone gave us a small bust of a cowboy as a wedding present. We both loved that little bust. It was dropped and broke into several pieces. Steve had the patience and aptitude to glue the thing back together. As he did it, he remarked, "I'm trying to put the pieces of your Cowboy back together." I remember when he said it, it gave me pause. I sensed the double entendre. I regret not pressing that point a bit. In retrospect, it was a foreshadowing of all that was to come.

By June 4th, the pull of the demon of alcoholism became too much to fight and he returned to the barracks. I firmly believe that the prayers of the saints were answered. Steve just chose to be disobedient again.

"I'm moving back to the barracks today," he told me. "Even though I broke it off with Jenifer, the pain is too great. I can't stand the idea that in four years' time I'm still going to see her face, still going to want to be with her, but be with you." He continued, "I looked at myself in the mirror the other day and asked myself, 'Did I just snap?' I do love you. It's there. It's just not the same. I'm tired of living a lie. I'm tired of being the husband you expect me to be. There's two people in here. I'm tired of being someone I'm not."

Chapter 5
Lean Into The Grief

*"It's too hard to look into your eyes and know what
I'm doing to you."*

God's Provision

I didn't take the news with grace and dignity. Once it became
evident he was leaving, I walked into the kitchen. A sense of
rage came over me; an anger that went to the depth of my soul.
I stepped over to the kitchen counter, put my arm parallel to the
small appliances on the counter and with a wide sweeping mo-
tion, pushed them all on to the floor. A primitive l roar escaped
my throat. My entire body was trembling. Steve came running
into the kitchen to find me throwing things across the room. He
had never seen me like that. Shoot, *I'd* never seen me like that.
The emotional roller coaster he had me on suddenly became
more than I could bear. I'm pretty sure I screamed some choice
words at him, although I have no memory of what I said.

He stayed until I calmed down. He actually put the items back on the counter for me. Amazingly, nothing broke. As he left, he looked at me and said, "It's too hard to look into your eyes and know what I'm doing to you."

I had little contact with Steve over the next 30 days. He took me off the bank account. We started talking through a separation agreement once again. Since Steve was planning to get out of the Army in early July, he was allowing me to take advantage of the move the Army would provide. This was scheduled for July 1st. I began packing. Gina threw a going away party. I counted the many ways God was providing for me.

Imagine if you will, that I didn't call Steve at the Chicago airport. What if I just went to Raleigh and surprised him at the gate. There's a pretty high likelihood I wouldn't have learned the reality of what went on. Imagine that a few short weeks after his tryst in Portland, Oregon, we moved there. Portland was the city where his mistress was. It was a place where I knew no one and where there would be no support system. God intervened and led me to make choices that protected me from this potential scenario.

Because I was obedient to God's leading, this all unfolded in a community where we both had support. We had amazing Christian friends who came along side us and helped us, prayed for us, talked with us, listened to us. We had Pastors that intervened and a Chaplain who got involved.

In a conversation with one of our pastors, he said to me, "This very well may be God's way of protecting you from a horrible life with Steve that revolves around alcohol."

I wasn't sure if this was true or not. I still held out hope that God would restore our marriage. I certainly believed He could.

At the same time, if the pastor was right, I'd seen enough to realize unless he was sober, I wanted no part of life with Steve.

My physical needs were being met. I was able to stay in military housing for a time. The military required him to give me a little bit of money each month for basic necessities. Additionally, I learned in North Carolina a couple must be legally separated for one year before the state will grant them a divorce. This meant I would have health care, and a small income for twelve months. Had this happened in Oregon, none of this would be the case. Realizing God's hand in all of this gave me much gratitude.

On June 19, I noted Psalm 100 in my journal.

"Shout joyfully to the Lord, all the earth.

Serve the Lord with gladness: Come before Him with joyful singing.

Know that the Lord Himself is God:

It is He who has made us, and not we ourselves:

We are His people and the sheep of His pasture.

Enter His gates with Thanksgiving

And His courts with praise.

Give Thanks to Him, Bless His name.

For the Lord is good;

His lovingkindness is everlasting

And His faithfulness to all generations."

Having my physical and emotional needs met by God, gave me the space to look at the reality of the situation. I came to understand just how sick my husband was; mentally, spiritually, emotionally, and physically. Further, I had a lot of time on my hands to take personal inventory of *my* emotional and mental health.

Our good Chaplain friend challenged me. He spoke truth in love by saying, "Audrey, as I've watched you walk through this, I've observed a few behaviors that I would describe as co-dependent. I think you would benefit from getting some counseling."

So, I did. I met several times with another fine Chaplain. One of the major things this Chaplain did was give me perspective. I had this idea that I was incomplete somehow without this man in my life and that I just couldn't go on without Steve. The Chaplain almost laughed out loud when I made this statement. When you consider what a strong, independent woman God made me to be, it is pretty darn funny. But, without *saying* what a load of hooey this was, he basically told me what a load of hooey it was. He helped me recognize this was a lie. Once I accepted the truth, that I didn't need this man, or any other for that matter, to have a fulfilled life, the building blocks were laid to move forward in healing.

On June 13th I noted in my journal and my Bible Job:23:10-12.

"But He knows the way I take; When He has tried me, I shall come forth as gold. My foot has held fast to His path; I have kept His way and not turned aside. I have not departed from the command of His lips; I have treasured the words of His mouth more than my necessary food."

Verse twelve especially resonated with me. I was at a healthy weight when this started. I lost 16 pounds in just one-month time. I had to force myself to eat. It could take me 45 minutes just to eat a single sandwich. I needed God more than I needed food. I clung to God. I was in constant prayer. Friends remarked my face glowed. I didn't understand how I could be in so much emotional pain and yet have so much peace at the same time. Further, I was determined that Marilyn's prayer would be answered and that I would get to the other side of this trial with no regrets.

The Hail Mary

Even though I had tremendous joy and peace, I knew I needed to forgive Steve. I'm not a jealous person. I readily forgave him for the actual acts of infidelity, lying to me over the years about other acts of adultery and drinking episodes, even having an affair with this woman in Oregon. In fact, at one point in the whole ordeal, before he broke it off with her, I called her and had a conversation with her. I wanted her to know I was a real person, that I loved my husband and there wasn't room for three in this marriage. She was intent on being with him.

"Well, let me just caution you my dear, if he cheated on me, he'll probably cheat on you. I'd think twice about it if I were you," I told her. It was a very calm conversation on both sides. I was prayed up and ready to have that chat without being emotional.

Where I struggled to forgive was for the hurt he was causing me. How could the man who pledged before God to love and cherish me for the rest of his life do this to me? I also struggled to forgive him for throwing away everything he believed to be good and right. I had trouble forgiving him for being the kind of man that would cheat on his wife. Lastly, I struggled to forgive myself for choosing a man with these weaknesses to be my husband. I'm a pretty smart gal and waited until I was close to 30 years old to marry. One would think an older woman would have the ability to choose a better mate than I had. This caused me to doubt myself, and my decisions, for a couple of years. My friend Dave told me that women tend to internalize the rejection of divorce much more than men do. Truth. It can be crippling if not dealt with.

On June 30th Steve called me and told me he was being given the opportunity to re-enlist, even though that window had long since closed. He was days away from starting his terminal leave, the amount of vacation days one has left at the end of one's enlistment. There was a special program in place and his chain of command offered the opportunity to him. He decided to take them up on it and he asked me to stay at Ft. Bragg. He told me he'd made an appointment with the counseling pastor at our church, and he asked me if he could come home. He also invited me to attend his re-enlistment ceremony the following day.

We had to act quickly to get the move cancelled. Since he was re-enlisting, there was no move courtesy from Uncle Sam. I was there when they opened on July 1st with a copy of his orders. I agreed to let him move back home. I was hopeful, but not optimistic, this would end differently than the last time. Later that day, I went to his re-enlistment ceremony. Vern administered the oath. Pam and Jason were also there. All of us held a small glimmer of hope this would bring about change for him and our marriage.

We picked up his things at the barracks afterwards and went home for the long July 4th weekend. There were some bitter-sweet moments over the next few days. A lot of tears were shed by both of us. We struggled to find 'safe' topics of conversation. The strain between us was so thick it would have taken a butcher knife to cut through it. We attended the fireworks celebration at Ft. Bragg July 4th with Pam and Vern.

Steve left the morning of July 5th and I didn't see him again until Monday morning July 8th. It was hard watching him walk out that door, knowing full well what he was doing and why he was leaving. He took the car, so I was without transportation all weekend. He didn't just let *me* down again, he really screwed up at work. He oversaw the arms room at his unit at the time. Monday morning was a scheduled inspection and he was a no show. The unit gave him a suspended article 15. Article 15's are non-judicial punishment mechanism that allows the chain of command to punish a soldier without a court martial. He was also given extra duty and two weeks restriction, meaning when he wasn't on duty or doing extra duty tasks he was to be at home. Lastly he was given a command referral to the Army's Drug and Alcohol program. The official reading of the sentencing was not read until July 14th. On July 13th Steve let me know he was planning to be gone all weekend again. That was it for me. I invited him to leave. He moved his things back to the barracks, which is where they restricted him for the next two weeks.

Grappling With Grief

Through the last few weeks of July and into early August, I was studying James 1:1-4.

2"Consider it all joy my brethren, when you encounter various trials, 3 Knowing that the testing of your faith produces endurance. 4 And let endurance have it's perfect result, that you may be perfect and complete, lacking in nothing."

I wrote this in my journal on August 7th.

Tonight I finished my study of James 1:1-4. I saw several things I want to get in this journal. These verses instruct the Christian in an appropriate Christian attitude and response when trials are encountered. One should cooperate in the circumstances under the authority of the Lord. According to Vines dictionary, this is the definition of JOY! This so we can be complete, leaving every grace present in Christ being manifested in us as a believer.

An attitude such as this would set us apart from non-Christians. In my current situation, I have recognized the truth of James 1:2-4., but still long for the trial to end, the pain to stop and for the blessing to come. The result of embracing the trial and 'just going with it' is that I am being perfected by God through this process. I need to let endurance have its perfect result.

I recognize that to continue to embrace the trial means to continue to work on my emotional issues and recovery. This will be a process that could take years. Probably will. It also means facing the fact that I need to be uninvolved with men in any complicated way for another several months. I'm frightened by this but am generally okay with it. I choose taking care of myself for a while over doing a band-aid remedy for loneliness. I can have companionship but want no ties to anyone for a while. My wounds are too raw – the pain is too sharp.

God alone is sufficient. For now, I am Christ's bride and He is my bridegroom. Glory be to God!

Clinging so desperately to God's truth made me realize I could no longer live in this horrible limbo. I needed to move forward with my life as if Steve was never going to get better – as if he was never going to change and sober up. I wrote a long letter to him expressing my sense of loss, disappointment, and grief. I communicated how unexpected this was from him. With what we had and what we'd shared it was really hard to wrap my mind around the 'new' Steve. I also wanted to let him know that I'd made the decision to leave North Carolina. The last paragraph of the letter read:

The day you told me you were an alcoholic, I remember telling you that I didn't want to live that life. This is still true. I don't have the strength to see anymore. That's partly why I'm leaving as soon as I can. It hurts too much to watch this tragedy unfold. Should you ever get yourself together, you'll know where to find me. I'll be getting on with my life, getting over you, getting past the pain and becoming the woman God is calling me to be. Just thought you should know how I feel. It will be the Lord Jesus who walks this angel home.

I stopped into the barracks to tell him I was leaving and give him the letter. He was having a small party. A single guy from the unit who was his roommate was there and about six others. There was a woman there with an elementary school aged child. I asked to speak to Steve alone in the hallway. He reluctantly followed me out. I told him of my decision and that I would likely be leaving by months end. He agreed this was best for both of us. I then asked who the woman was.

"She's the woman I'm dating. Her name is Beth. That's her daughter with her," he said matter-of-factly.

"Where did you meet her?" I asked

"The Palomino," he responded. "I met her July fourth weekend."

"Wait, what?" I barked. "You've been seeing her an entire month?"

He simply shrugged and walked back into his barracks room.

If I thought I was angry before, I was really angry now. I decided I would work on continued forgiveness in the future. I needed to be angry to have the strength to leave town and start a new life in a new community. The old saying is, "Hell hath no fury like a woman scorned." Twice scorned? Shut the front door and get out of the way!

Even though I was angry, I was still grieving.

I grieved the loss of a dream. I grieved the loss of the life I had known before. I grieved the loss of the sweetness between us. It's a funny thing, grief. Your whole body screams with pain. The ache in your soul is so great. It's hard to understand how life can go on around you. And yet it does. People laugh. People get sick. Babies are born. People go to work. The sun rises and sets. It rains. It snows. The seasons change. The world marches on. It does not stop for your pain, as it seems it should.

The pain feels like your soul is in a vice grip that you're sure will never give. And yet it does. One millimeter at a time the vice grip lifts its hold. You pry one finger at a time, until one day, it gives completely.

But alas, your soul is forever shaped by where the clench of your grief was held in the vice grip. You rejoin life. You go to work. You laugh. You watch the sun rise and set. You feel the rain on your face and marvel at the snow. You feel something other than the clench of the vice grip of your grief. You hear the music. You play the music. You *are* the music! Life goes on around you with you in it once again.

If you lean into the grip of grief hard, the vice grip shakes loose faster. It's not that time heals the wound, it's what you do with the time that matters. Feel the grip. Grieve the grief. The pain is a gift.

Chapter 6
Moving Back To Colorado

**"You're just the one who gets left.
I'm the one who does the leaving."**

Moving Prep

Initially, the plan was Steve would help me move to Colorado. He would drive the U-Haul. I would drive the car. It became apparent as the days wore on this was beyond foolish. After a lot of prayer and research, I determined I could do it myself. I got counsel from my friends, Dave and Marilyn, as well. Dave and I talked through the logistics of it. He was sure I had the ability to pull this off. The largest U-Haul truck was automatic. I could rent a trailer and haul the car. If I didn't have to back up, I could do this.

August 21st found me flying west to Colorado Springs, Colorado. I was on a recon mission to find a place to live. I rented a car at the airport and drove to my friend Margie's house. Margie and her family were dear friends we attended church with before moving to North Carolina. She was gracious to let me stay in their spare bedroom for the few days I was in town. Finding a place to rent with no income turned out to be a bit trickier than I expected. The first couple of places I applied turned me down cold since I was currently unemployed.

On August 24th, I found a little house in Security, Colorado, a bedroom community to Colorado Springs and just minutes from Ft. Carson. I prayed for wisdom and for God to show me when I found the right place. The house was surrounded by giant oak trees. As I was waiting for the landlord to arrive so I could see the interior, I was struck by those trees and how much shade they would provide in the summer months. As I waited in the rental car, I was reading from my '*Streams in the Desert I*' devotional. The premise of the reading was how light gets through the darkness and makes things grow, in the physical sense and in the spiritual sense. The final line said, "Where there is much light, there is much shade." I looked again at those strong, protective oak trees and the shade they provided. I had a powerful impression this was a word from the Lord. This was where I was to live.

The landlord arrived and I saw the interior of the house. It wasn't the Ritz, but it provided everything I needed and everything I had prayed for except a dishwasher. There was a fenced back yard for my dogs. The best part was there was no grass! I wouldn't have to worry about my dogs destroying the lawn. I'd prayed for plenty of storage. There were three bedrooms, so one whole room would be my storage. I'd prayed for a washer/dryer hookup. It had that right off the kitchen. The kitchen was a hideous Pepto Bismol pink with red indoor/outdoor carpet. The durable carpet was a blessing as the kitchen was on the same side of the house as the back yard. Those muddy paw prints would clean right up and the walls and cupboards could be painted.

After the interior viewing, I followed the landlord to his home to complete the application and put down my deposit. The other apartments were owned by corporations. This time, I was dealing directly with the owner of the property. I filled everything out and as I did, I realized if I was going to get this house, I would have to dig deep into my sales skills. I needed to sell this guy on *me*. I laid the pen down and looked the man in the eye.

"Sir," I said, "I don't have a job yet. I will start looking as soon as I get moved here. I have the money today for the first month's rent and the deposit. My husband is in the Army and I am guaranteed an amount of money per month for at least a year. That amount is enough to cover the rent. I'm a farm and ranch girl from South Dakota. I was raised to work hard and pay my bills. I will pay you your rent on time, every month. I'm asking you to take a risk on me and let me rent this place from you."

I held his gaze. He looked at me for what seemed like an eternity. Then he smiled.

"I don't usually do this sort of thing, but I believe you and I think you will be a good tenant. I'm going to take the risk," he said warmly.

The little house on Frontier Drive in Security, Colorado was mine!

The landlord told me the current tenant would be out on Aug 30th and I was welcome to take possession of the rental that afternoon. I flew back to North Carolina the afternoon of the 24th. Since I was planning to depart by August 27th, there was much to accomplish in just two days. I secured packing boxes and moving blankets, then began the process of packing up my household goods.

On the 26th, Steve came over at my request. I showed him where his things were in the house and gave him my address so he could mail me the monthly basic allowance for housing (BAH). This is what the military required him provide me as long as we were married. It was enough to cover my rent in Colorado. This was a huge blessing and certainly part of God's provision as I made this transition! I had some things I wanted to say to him.

"I want you to know I'm not sorry I married you. I don't regret it. I loved you. I miss you and miss having you in my life. Up until all of this happened, I thought you were a good husband to me," I told him.

He made no response. I asked him if he had anything he wanted to say to me. He shrugged.

"I'm sorry I guess. Look, you're just the one who gets left. I'm the one who does the leaving. You're the one who gets all the hugs and sympathy. I get all the anger and disapproval," he said lamely.

Despite that pitiful response, I hugged him good-bye and watched him drive away in his new Dodge Ram pickup. I have never seen him again.

Later that day Dave, Marilyn, Pam, Vern, Gina, Jason and one other woman from our Bible Study, Caroline, all spent the evening loading my household goods into the U-Haul. The men got my car on the trailer. I said my good- byes to all but Marilyn and Dave as I was sleeping at their house that night. There weren't enough words to thank these good friends for all the love and support they'd given me through the most difficult time of my life.

"I've never experienced friendship like you all have shown me. It is incredibly special to me. I hope God provides me the opportunity to be that kind of friend to someone else one day," I said through my tears.

I fed the dogs, Fly and OD, and put some extra water out for them in their dog run. The plan was to pick them up in the morning on the way out of town. Then, I got behind the wheel of the biggest truck U-Haul makes, pulling my Grand Am and drove to Dave and Marilyn's. They fed me. Marilyn and I visited for a bit and then we all turned in early. Tomorrow would be a long day.

On the morning of August 27th, just four months after this ordeal began, I said good-bye to Ft. Bragg, North Carolina, home of the Airborne. Fly and OD were on the seat next to me. I had a ball cap on my head in an effort to look tougher than I felt. With Mindy McCready's "A Girl's Gotta Do (What a Girl's Gotta Do)" blaring on the cassette player and a determined look on my face I drove out of town. He might be willing to ruin his life, but he wasn't taking me down with him. I was moving on.

Heading West

We (the dogs and I) drove to Nashville the first day. I found a pet friendly hotel with a parking lot that went all the way around the hotel. This was important, because I had no idea how to back that beast up with the car and trailer on the back. I called Marilyn and Dave to let them know I was in for the night. I fed and watered the dogs. I was asleep before my head touched the pillow. The next day I drove to Norman, Oklahoma. I spent the night with my brother Patrick and his wife.

Day three of my journey West, August 29th found me in Agate, Colorado, just a couple hours east of Colorado Springs with my niece and her husband. The following morning my niece asked if I wanted to take the portable dishwasher they had. My parents had given it to them a few years before and they no longer needed it. I just smiled and said yes, thinking it was just like God to show up and show off. The last thing I prayed for in my new Colorado home was provided.

On the afternoon of August 30th, my friend Margie, her husband and their three strong sons helped me unload the massive U-Haul. They hooked up my washer and dryer, set up my bed and got my car off the trailer. I took them out to pizza as a thank you. I returned the U-Haul, trailer and blankets on the 31st. And even a few boxes that hadn't been used. I spent Sunday and Labor Day Monday unpacking and setting up my home.

From this day forward my life became about healing, moving forward and forging a new life in Colorado. My daily success and failure in that is evidenced in my journal entries. There were good days and bad days. I wrote this on September 4, 1997.

I haven't been to church or a Bible study for two weeks now. How I hunger and thirst to sing praises, hear the Word and fellowship with other believers. Thank you God for that hunger, that drive, that all-encompassing need to spend time with you and be in your presence.

You spoke to me today! I was getting all wrapped around the axle as to how I'm going to pay my bills next month. You very clearly said, "Don't be anxious my child."

I was filled with such a comforting warmth and felt tears of joy and gratitude well up inside of me. Last night, you comforted me. I was very tired and feeling quite lonely. I prayed and asked you to comfort me and to fill up that loneliness with your Spirit. I could feel the loneliness seep out of my spirit and felt You seep in. What an awesome experience! I don't know how you did it Lord, but you did, and I praise you for it.

Lord, I am seeking your wisdom, your guidance and your direction in my job search. You tell me in your Word tonight in Psalm 16:11, 'Thou wilt make known to me the path of life.' These are David's words and I claim them for myself. Please tell me the path I should take Lord. You know even better than I my needs. Jehovah Jireh, I am counting on you. I pray Lord, not one bill would go unpaid and I will have every penny I need to live in the coming weeks and months. You also gave me Proverbs 4:26 tonight, "Watch the path of your feet and all your ways will be established."

Lord, thank you for my dogs. I am so grateful for their companionship. I'm sure this house is where you wanted me. Thank you for bringing me here. You are so faithful and true. I praise you because you are worthy.

This was a good day.

Chapter 7
This Is From Me

"I'm going to kill you."

God Heals

Driving around Colorado Springs as I settled in was surprisingly difficult. The thing I hadn't expected was the memories being back ignited. It seemed there was a memory on every corner. I was comforted some knowing this was normal. In my last session with the counseling Chaplain, he cautioned me about how grief works.

"You'll go days without crying, then suddenly a sound, a smell or a memory will come out of nowhere and knock you down. This is normal. Just go with it and you'll be fine," he explained.

I was so grateful for that insight. Without it I believe I would have questioned my 'progress'. There is no right or wrong way to grieve loss. I, being a person of action and always moving forward, needed to understand, for me, those memories and those bad days were part of the grief process.

I found a new home church. The church I chose was a non-denominational church that preached from the Bible and believed in spreading the good news about Jesus. It was a large church, but I knew a handful of people who attended already. Some I knew were former co-workers at JA and others, like Margie and her husband, I knew from the little church on Flying W Ranch. Seeing a few familiar faces on Sunday was comforting. Another reason I chose the church, was because of a conversation I overheard between one of the two senior pastors and a parishioner the first Sunday I visited the church. The pastor was sharing his heart for single women in the church. His care and concern were moving to me considering my situation.

I signed up and took a grief recovery workshop. This was probably the single most important step I took on my road to healing. I learned so many things about grief and the grief process. Some things I already knew, but I learned new things too. The biggest 'new' concept I learned was that grief is often undelivered communication. That would become a big deal later.

I looked up the Fellowship of Christian Cowboys chapter we'd started prior to moving three years before and was thrilled to find it was still up and running! I learned when I started going to the meetings, that the chapter had dwindled down to just one person for a time in our absence. That man remained faithful for a full year, showing up at the advertised meeting place and time. He used that time to pray and study the Lord's word. Then, one week, someone came. The next week, that person brought a friend. Then a few more came. By the time I started attending again, there were about a dozen members. I was astonished at that one man's faith and faithfulness.

I joined a woman's Bible study my friend Margie was hosting in her home. We were a small group. It was nice to have weekly connection with other women. We prayed for each other and encouraged one another.

Margie was a Biblical counselor. I started sessions with her after the six-week grief recovery workshop was completed. We talked about how I was doing week-to-week and we also focused on spiritual truths and my personal spiritual growth. There was one day that was revolutionary for me, and it had nothing to do with my divorce. I don't remember what we were discussing or how we even got around to this topic, but Margie made the statement that women who are raped often act out by becoming sexually promiscuous. She knew nothing about what happened to me. I just stared at her. I was speechless. I consider myself a smart person and yet, I had never put together my ten years of going down the wrong path was a direct result of experiencing date rape.

The emotions I felt in that moment came like a flood. I felt relieved. The choices I made years before were a normal reaction to a horrible wrong I'd experienced. I felt validated. Much like when I saw the movie on date rape years before and found what happened to me had a name, I realized that I wasn't ruined or damaged, I had been trying to deal with the emotional pain of what was taken from me.

"Are you okay?" Margie asked.

"I lost my virginity in a date rape in college," I stammered. "Can't believe I never put it together that was why I went down the path I did."

The realization of the truth was so overwhelming that I fell silent. Margie ended the session early, as I was clearly processing this newfound truth. Looking back on it now, I realize this was God's grace in action. Even though I'd turned away from that of life years before and I knew I was forgiven, I still carried the shame of it all. God doesn't just paint over our sin, he removes it. Psalm 103:12 says,

> "As far as the east is from the west, So far has He removed our transgressions from us."

He went to the cross for my sin and for yours, dear reader. He became sin so we can be free from the burden of it. What a loving, caring, healing God of truth we serve. He loved me so much, he wanted to squash a lie I'd believed for years. There was no need to be ashamed. I was completely and totally forgiven for my past.

God Speaks

I found a part time seasonal job that would help me pay the bills until I could find full time work in my field. The work was noon to six Tuesday through Saturday. This gave me all day Monday and four hours Tuesday through Friday to job hunt. The economy was down in Colorado Springs. Someone told me it took the average person six months to find work. I was very blessed to find a job in my field by late November. Though I didn't start the job until January 1st, I felt grateful for God's provision.

I had little contact with Steve. He did call from time to time whenever something was happening with him that affected me or that we had to discuss. He refused to send me the monthly BAH. He told me I was going to have to take him to court to get the money, which was baloney, as the Army required it. Since we had a written separation agreement, filed with the state of North Carolina, I decided to work with his chain of command instead. I reached out to his First Sergeant and informed him of the situation. The First Sergeant agreed to help me and take it up with Steve. In working with the First Sergeant, I learned the holdup was that Steve never cleared the housing we were living in. From the Army's point of view, he still had on post quarters other than the barracks. Thus, the Army wasn't able to provide the BAH.

What happened next blew me away. Angry I had contacted his unit over the owed money, I got a call from Steve on November 19 and this is what he said.

"I'm going to kill you. I've been thinking about using a sniper rifle from 1000 feet away to blow that pretty little head off. You better watch your back. I know people in Colorado. Being in North Carolina, no one would ever suspect me. I have leave coming up and I'm thinking about driving out there and taking care of it myself. I promise you it will be slow and painful," he said angrily.

He threatened to kill the dogs too. While the threats were frightening, they also broke my heart. I was so sad this man who pledged to God in our wedding ceremony that he would provide for me and protect me for the rest of my life was now threatening my life. I don't think hiring an assassin was what he meant when he asked God to walk this angel home. The honest, caring, loving man I once knew had become an angry, self-centered, hateful man. This is what addiction does to people.

I wrote this in my journal on November 20th.

> *I had a rough night last night. It was so painful to hear all his accusations and threats. He believes I called his First Sergeant for vindictive purposes. It's impossible to convey to one who is so mentally and emotionally ill that it causes me great pain to do the difficult thing of holding him accountable for his actions. My motives are*

not selfish. My actions are for Steve. I do him no favors by letting him off the hook. Last week, I laid awake for two nights until at least 2 a.m. agonizing and crying over the fact that involving his chain of command or taking any legal action will in the short-term be painful and uncomfortable to him. He perceives it as hurting him and that hurts me…deeply.

I have fully forgiven Steve thanks to God's grace. The anger and resentment I once had for him is gone. Praise be to God. It has been replaced with pity for the state he's in. Any romantic love I had for him is also gone, but my heart is full of Christ's love toward him as a hurting human being. I pray for him daily and trust God will restore him to right relationship to Himself in time. The glory will be the Lords.

Today I'm reading in I Corinthians Chapter 5:11. Paul tells the Corinthians to remove sinners from their midst and to not associate with these so-called brothers.

"But actually, I wrote to you not to associate with any so-called brother if he should be an immoral person, or covetous, or an idolater, or a reviler, or a drunkard, or swindler – not even to eat with such a one."

For application, I think I need to avoid these phone conversations with Steve. They are upsetting to me and only feed his anger as I refuse to be drawn in. At one-point last night I did become angry and he loved it. He wants to provoke me, to push my buttons, scare me and manipulate me.

*Thank you God that YOU are my protector, my refuge
and my fortress.*

This wasn't just a bad day; it was a bad week.

It took until January for the BAH to get sorted out, but it finally did. Even though I'd started my job, it was a financial blessing to have that little bit of extra cash coming in every month. I used it to pay off a little credit card debt and replenish my depleted savings account. I told the First Sergeant about the threats, but I don't think he took it very seriously. I do think it motivated him to get the financial issue squared away so he didn't have to deal with it further.

As a result of the frightening phone call, I took different routes home every day. I always looked around the parking lot when leaving my office or a work site. I approached my little rental property very carefully and looked for any cars I didn't recognize and especially any with a North Carolina license plate. If I saw a vehicle I didn't recognize, I would drive slowly by, take a good look at it and then come back a different way. I spoke to a member of the law enforcement community about the possibility of getting a handgun for protection. He advised against it and asked me an especially important question.

"Audrey, if Steve were coming through the door or window uninvited, would you be able to shoot to kill?" he asked.

I was quiet for a moment, then responded, "That is an excellent question and I have to say the answer would be no. This is my husband. Despite everything, I couldn't do that to him."

"Then don't get a gun," he said. "You're more likely to be killed with your own weapon by an intruder, no matter who they are, if you're not comfortable enough to shoot to kill."

That settled that. As it turned out, he never materialized anyway, and months went by before I heard anything from him again. I celebrated Christmas with my family in South Dakota. I started my new job as the first female professional ever hired at the Pikes Peak Council of the Boy Scouts of America in January. I got a lot of sideways looks in 1998 as a chick in a Boy Scout uniform. The job was very demanding of my time and talents. It was good for me to be busy though. I was making new friends at church and through the Fellowship of Christian Cowboys. I was moving forward, and my heart was healing some, but I was stuck. I still hoped and prayed for reconciliation. I didn't believe God had released me from the marriage. We were, after all, still legally married. The God I love and serve is in the miracle business. I was counting on a miracle.

On February 1, 1998 I read the devotional from *'Streams in the Desert I'*. This is what it said in part.

"This thing is from me (I Kings 12:24)

Life's disappointments are veiled love's appointments.
Rev C.A. Fox

My child, I have a message for you today, let me whisper it in your ear, that it may gild with glory any storm clouds which may arise, and smooth the rough places upon which you may have to tread. It is short, only five words, but let them sink into your inmost soul: use them as a pillow upon which to rest your weary head. This thing is from ME.

Have you ever thought of it, that all that concerns you concerns Me too? For, 'he that toucheth you, toucheth the apple of mine eye' (Zech 2:8). You are very precious in

My sight (Isa. 43:4). Therefore, it is My special delight to educate you.

Are you passing through a night of sorrow? This thing is from Me. I am the Man of Sorrows and acquainted with grief. I have let earthly comforters fail you, that by turning to Me you may obtain everlasting consolation (2 Thess 2:16-17).

This day I place in your hand this pot of holy oil. Make use of it, free My child. Let every circumstance that arises, every word that pains you, every interruption that would make you impatient, every revelation of your weakness be anointed with it. The sting will go as you learn to see Me in all things.

Laura A. Barter Snow

This is from Me, the Savior said,

As bending low He kissed my brow,

For One who loves you thus has led.

Just rest in Me, be patient now,

Your Father knows you have need of this,

Tho', why perchance you cannot see

Grieve not for things you've seemed to miss

The thing I send is best for thee.

Then, looking through my tears, I plead,

Dear Lord, forgive, I did not know,

'Twoll not be hard since Thou dost treat,

Each path before me here below.

And for my good this thing must be,

His grace sufficient for each test.

So still I'll sing, 'Whatever be

God's way for me is always best.'"

This reading got my attention. It seemed God was assuring me that this valley I was in, this place I was walking, this trial, was from God. It was filtered through his loving fingers and was His best for me. I recalled what my pastor told me months earlier about this being God's way of protecting me from a horrible life with Steve that revolved around alcohol. Maybe this really was from God.

Later that morning, I had a Christian radio station on. I never, ever listened to this particular station, but my friend Margie had told me that I should listen to the Dr. David Jeremiah show. I tuned in just for that and was listening to the sermon with half an ear. I was walking down the hallway away from the stereo in the living room when I heard him say, *"This thing is from Me. My child, I have a message for you today...."*

I stopped. I listened. Did I hear that right?

I slowly walked back into the living room and listened as the reading continued. *"...let me whisper it in your ear, that it may gild with glory any storm clouds which may arise and smooth the rough places upon which you may have to tread.*

I grabbed the devotional book. *"It is short, only five words..."*

I sank to my knees devotional in hand. *"...but let them sink into your inmost soul: use them as a pillow upon which to rest your weary head."*

I hurriedly opened the book to that days reading, just in time to hear him say, *"This is from ME."*

I read along, on my knees in front of the stereo with tears streaming down my face as Dr. David Jeremiah recited the entire reading I'd read just a few hours earlier. This was a clear message from God. He allowed this mess into my life to protect me. Knowing the situation was from God didn't make it hurt any less. It did give me peace. I came to understand, God had my best in mind. As Marilyn told me months earlier in the wee hours of the morning when the crisis began, I was learning that God is Sovereign, and that God *alone* is sovereign.

Chapter 8
Released

"I do the best in the middle of chaos.
If I don't have it, I create my own."

Rebellion

Being 'separated' is a weird marital status. Not single. Not together. As a Christian woman, I still considered myself married. I'm also human. I was lonely and a bit depressed. I wrote this in my journal on March 25th.

"God, I want to be free of this pain. I want to feel whole again…not like there is a hole in my heart. This wound is so deep, so painful, almost debilitating in its acuteness. I feel a subtle depression set over me whenever I'm alone. I want to let go of this marriage, but you've told me to wait, to not give up, to hang on for the last half hour. Today I am faithfully following you and letting you fight for my marriage. God, help me to remain steady on your path. I feel so sad, so heavy, so unhappy, so lonely, SOOO not

where I want to be in life. I understand I am here for your
purpose and I'm okay with that. It's just so HARD here.
Lord, prepare me for deliverance and healing. Show me
and guide me. I love you God. I pray that now as I go to
sleep, you will cause my sleep to be sweet."

On April 6th I had a prayer day. God showed me that I was letting a lot of things rob my joy. My pride was causing me to desperately want to 'save' my marriage. I told myself I wanted a miracle for God to be glorified. While that was mostly true, the real underlying cause was I wanted to win, to be right. I also realized I wanted Steve to leave the woman he was currently seeing to punish her for taking away my husband.

God showed me I had waivered in my faith in His sovereignty. He really did have my best in mind despite how it looked. The Lord convicted me on my thought life. I was thinking a lot about how things would look if Steve chose reconciliation, or if he didn't. The thing God showed me is it didn't matter what Steve chose. God had a blessing and a promise in store for me. There was a greater purpose in God's plan for my life that was irrelevant to Steve's choices.

Additionally, I was stuck, replaying things I wanted to say to Steve but hadn't had the opportunity. Many were in response to horrid things he said to me in anger during the past few months. I felt compelled to defend myself or to communicate how he had hurt me but believed I would never get the chance to say what I wanted to say. Knowing that grief is largely undelivered communication made it frustrating. This one area was increasingly difficult for me to overcome. I prayed for a way for these tapes in my head to stop.

The final thing the Lord showed me on that prayer day was I really wanted Steve to 'do the right thing' so he could be right with God and have a life of happiness and peace. God showed me in that prayer time this was not something I needed to concern myself with. That was between God and Steve. I only needed to be concerned with *my* life, *my* relationship with the Lord and his plan form *me*.

Often, after a mountain top experience there is a valley. Although God showed me all of this in April, I still wanted what I wanted. I *expected* God to give me a miracle and save my marriage. Even after he had so plainly told me, "This is from Me," I still expected Him to bend His will to mine. Even with the insight and wisdom God gave me into my incorrect thinking, I refused to give myself over to His will. That stubborn streak of the one who ate the cookies and drove seven miles in impassable mud rose up. I was dangerously close to becoming hard-hearted towards God. I was still focused on being right and getting my way.

I got a call from Steve soon after this prayer date. The woman he was seeing was pregnant again. She became pregnant the first time when I was still in North Carolina. They aborted that baby. This one they would keep and raise together. He was informing me he would be filing for a divorce as soon as the state of North Carolina would allow. That would be the middle of July. Of course, now there was a child. His place was with his new family.

I got mad. I got mad at God. I shut myself off from God. I didn't pray. I didn't have a quiet time. I didn't go to church as much and when I did, I wouldn't take communion because I had sin in my life, and I was purposely choosing not to deal with it. I started hanging out at Cowboys on Saturday evenings.

I had a few offers to go on dates and took a couple of the young cowboys up on their offer. I let things go too far. The song had gone out of my life. There was no joy, no hope, and no contentment. There was only loneliness, pain, and sorrow. For about six weeks, I flirted with my old lifestyle. It was bleak and dark.

On May 9th, exactly one year to the day from picking Steve up at the Raleigh, North Carolina airport, I drove to South Dakota to spend the weekend with my parents. I prayed and cried most of the drive. I remember praying this prayer, "Okay God. I'm mad at you. I need you, but I'm still mad."

If you open the door to your heart just a crack, God will come in. That's all it took for His presence to come flooding back. He's a big God. He can handle our anger. It's a seven-hour drive each way to Hot Springs, South Dakota from Colorado Springs, Colorado. God and I had plenty of time to work things out. I repented of all the sin I'd let creep in. This excerpt from my journal May 10th shows all that God had for me once I opened myself back up to him.

> God showed me something important on the way to
> South Dakota yesterday. I was thinking that it's been one
> year. I've come a long way, still have a long way to go.
> For the most part, I have been faithful and though I have
> stumbled, I have trusted. Yet, the trial continues. I was
> hoping for a miracle, hoping for healing in my marriage.
> The outlook looks grim. I have stopped praying for Steve,
> for 'us". Having felt let down by God and angry at Him, I
> pulled away. I think at some level I believed that if I was
> faithful, God would grant me a miracle. I don't believe
> it's going to happen. I don't think that's a lack of faith. I
> think that's reality. God is protecting me from the sin in

Steve's life. What God showed me is this. The trial is not over because my faith is still being tested. He wants to know if I'll trust Him no matter what. He wants to know if I'll trust Him if Steve doesn't come back, if I'm alone, if I never have children, if I never re-marry…no matter what. Am I truly His child and willing to walk wherever He takes me, whether I want to go or not? He's testing my faith.

I haven't given Him an answer yet. The alternative seems so bleak. I want to be obedient, but am afraid I'll fail. Be overwhelmed with loneliness. I'm still working through this. God is calling me back. He misses me… and I Him. "Even if you do it wrong and miss the joy I've planned, I will never let go of your hand."

Closure

Right after this trip, I began to pray for an opportunity to communicate all of those tapes stuck in my head. But, I wanted to approach it differently than I had in the past year. I spent twelve months telling Steve everything he was doing wrong, pleading with him to change his mind and trying to will him to pull his head out of his butt. Never one time had I tried to understand his point of view. So, I asked God for the opportunity to first understand him and then maybe, just maybe I would be able to say the things I needed to say. If grief is undelivered communication, perhaps it would go a long way in healing my broken heart. In addition, if I could say out loud to him all those tapes stuck in my head, maybe they would quit playing once and for all.

On May 18th, I got a call from Steve. He called to tell me he was being kicked out of the Army for rehab failure. It would happen in July sometime. He wanted me to know as this would mean his financial commitment to me would end in July. After he communicated that message, I said a quick prayer and took a deep breath.

"Steve," I said, "I've spent the last year telling you you're wrong and why. I've never tried to understand your point of view. I'm sorry for that. I would really like to understand what happened and why you left."

Amazingly, that opened the floodgates. He told me everything. I just listened and asked questions. After a good bit of time, I was able to share a few things that I wanted to say. This would be the first of three such calls. I made notes so I wouldn't forget anything I needed to communicate. God gave me the tremendous gift of getting it all out! So much so, that as I pen this, I have no memory of what any of those things were. I have no idea what had me so worked up and stuck that I couldn't stop the tapes of what I wanted to say in my head. God provided a way for me to have complete and total cleansing and closure.

One of the topics Steve brought up on the third call was reconciliation. This surprised me more than a little. I entertained the idea with him to keep the conversation going. A couple days later, I wrote him a letter with the terms of reconciliation. I laid out ground rules that if he came to Colorado we would not live in the same house until he demonstrated a few months of sobriety and was able to support himself. Additionally, he and I would get individual counseling and then marriage counseling together. He would not move in with me until all counselors agreed it was a good idea.

Up to this point, nearly all decisions about our marriage had been imposed by Steve upon me. Establishing boundaries around a possible, even though highly improbably reconciliation was empowering. It felt good to have a voice and a choice.

A fourth and final call came a few days after he got this letter.

"I got your letter," he said. "I understand why you laid out those ground rules. You were smart to do that. But I can't. I'm too fragile right now to even try to do any of that. I do the best in the middle of chaos. If I don't have it, I create my own. I'm not going to put you through that."

"Well, I appreciate your honesty. I guess there's not much else to say, "I said.

"No, I guess not," he replied.

"So, I guess this is goodbye," I choked.

"Yes, I guess this is goodbye," he said.

"Good-bye Steve, I hope you have a good life. Good luck with the baby and take care of Beth," I said through my tears.

"Good-bye Audrey," he said, "I loved you."

"I loved you more," I said and slowly put the phone back in its cradle.

I've never spoken to him again.

I knew in that moment I was completely released from Steve by God. The divorce wouldn't be final until October, but at long last, God had released me. I was free to move on. As time went on, I came to understand not being released by God until then wasn't for the purpose of reconciliation. It was never about that. It was to protect me from doing more of what I did when I was mad at God. As long as I felt emotionally married, even though we weren't together, as a Christian woman I believed I couldn't freely date or move on with another man until God released me. God was protecting me from my own stupidity, once again.

Further, by having the divorce take so many months per North Carolina law, God was giving me not only financial provision, but health insurance and access to care at Ft. Carson. Also, I had all the privileges a military installation affords the active duty until the divorce was final. Or in this case, until he was discharged in July. Protecting and providing is what God does. It's who He is.

One Last Thing

We did have one final piece of business to conduct. Steve still owed me $2600 in support. It was clear I was never going to get that money, especially now that he was getting chaptered out of the Army. At the advice of my attorney, I dropped the complaint I'd filed with a North Carolina court for the delinquent alimony. Instead, I was keeping the entirety of our tax return, a total of $450 measly bucks.

I sent a letter to Steve in early June letting him know this. The attorney was copied, and I asked moving forward he only communicate with me through my attorney. It was all business. The personal was done.

One would think, at this point, there would be nothing left that could shock me. I believed we'd left things in a really good way and that things between us were resolved. I no longer harbored any ill will towards him. Mistakenly, I thought he felt the same way based on our final conversations. I was blindsided by what he did next. Drawing from his recent playbook, his response to the letter was to call my home and leave death threats for me and the dogs on the answering machine. A few days later, his pregnant girlfriend also called and left a threatening message. Both messages were recorded on tape.

Knowing the Army was about to release him, and he would be free to move about the country, I was extremely terrified. I made a copy of the tape and sent it to the unit. Remember, this was the 90's when answering machines actually had physical cassette tapes that recorded messages. The First Sergeant called me as soon as he heard the tape.

"Mrs. R," he said, "I wanted to first of all apologize. When you told me about the tape, I didn't expect it to amount to much. I was wrong. You have reason to be afraid. The Army is pressing charges against your husband. We're notifying him today."

"Thank you so much," I said. "And thank you for taking me seriously."

A couple of days later I got another phone call from the First Sergeant, "Mrs. R, I'm sorry to inform you that Sgt. R attempted suicide last night."

Strange things go through one's mind in a situation such as this. My first thought was *'attempted'. He said 'attempted'. That means Steve's not dead. No life insurance money.*

Somewhat aghast that my mind went first to that inappropriate thought, I managed to say something different than what I was thinking.

"So, he's alive?" I asked.

"Yes, but barely," the First Sergeant said. "He's in a coma at Womack Army Hospital. He'll probably survive. That woman he's dating showed up at the hospital. Since she's not family, they wouldn't let her see him. She created such a violent scene she had to be escorted off post by the Military Police (MP) and she has been permanently banned from ever coming on Ft. Bragg," he volunteered.

All I could say was, "Wow."

I was trying to imagine how bad her behavior must have been for her to be permanently banned from post. That is a profoundly serious and highly unusual action for the military to take. I surmised she must be as nuts as he had become.

"Would you mind notifying his parents?" the First Sergeant asked. "I hate to ask that of you, but you're still listed as his next of kin and legally I have to notify you."

"I don't mind. It's best it comes from me anyway," I replied.

When I called on July 16th to check the progress of the court martial, I found out he'd been separated from the Army an entire week! During our call, the First Sergeant told me they found letters in his room with more threats. According to him, these letters contained 'slanderous' things about me and the First Sergeant. I also learned he was on a psyche hold for a full week after he was released from the hospital.

The Criminal Investigation Department (CID) at Ft. Bragg investigated the charges against him. They determined it would be a waste of time to take him to court martial given his mental and emotional state. Consequently, the unit went ahead with removing him from active duty. The First Sergeant told me once the decision came down not to court martial him, the unit had him out processed and out of the Army in 24 hours. Typically, soldiers are given 30 days to out process. Getting the job done in 24 hours gives testament to how badly the Army wanted to be rid of this problem.

His last day in the Army was July 9th. No one from the unit had presence of mind to notify me. When I expressed concern for my safety to the First Sergeant he said, "He can't even stay sober long enough to get to work. There's no way he could get himself organized to drive to Colorado and make good on his threats. The Army made sure he was punished financially as well, so I doubt he would have the money to make the trip."

While this brought some comfort, I still got a restraining order for both of them in a Colorado Springs court. I only had to play a few words of the tape for the judge and he readily supplied the restraining orders. The next step was to get the orders served in North Carolina. When I called the County Sheriff I learned that I couldn't mail the restraining order to them to be served. The documents had to be delivered in person to the Sherrif's office. That was a problem, but I'm a problem solver. I knew any of my friends in Fayetteville would have delivered the papers for me. I had a better idea.

My work was sending me to Nashville, Tennessee for a week to attend a conference. I had some vacation time coming, so I decided to take a couple days off and fly from Nashville to Fayetteville. It would be great to catch up with my good friends who had done so much to help me the year before. While I was there, I borrowed a car and drove to the Sheriff's office in the next county. I hand delivered those restraining orders myself. Written notice arrived in my mailbox about a week later that Steve and Baby Mama had been served.

Chapter 9
Where Was God For Steve?

"I'm tired of living a lie. I'm tired of being the husband you expect me to be."

A Gentile and A Tax Collector

One of the things I really struggled with through the months and months this mess went on was where God was for Steve in it all. The spiritual battle he was in was so obvious.

As the men and our church walked him through the steps of spiritual discipline in May and June, the struggle was evidenced by things he said to them and to me. In the second step of the discipline, where two go, the Chaplain and Vern reported to me that he admitted to being disobedient to the Lord.

"I've grown weary of the struggle," he told them, "the struggle of rising above the old Steve and seeking to be a new creature in Christ."

A few days later, Steve and I were having a conversation. According to my journal notes, I think I was trying to 'reason' with him. This had about as much affect as reasoning with a two-year-old. I'm reminded of what the good Chaplain told me when he had the first conversation with Steve in step one of the spiritual discipline process.

"Audrey" he said, "there's no such thing as a fallen Christian, only disobedient ones."

In my conversation with Steve that day he told me the thing that hurt him the most was the disobedience to Christ.

"It brings tears to my eyes to willfully disobey," he said. He went on, "But, I'm tired of living a lie. I'm tired of being the husband you expect me to be. There's two people in here. I'm tired of being someone I'm not."

"You're quitting too soon," I answered, "I believe you're a better man than this. You are stronger and a man of greater integrity than this. Rangers don't leave a comrade behind. You got through Ranger school for the love of Pete. You're tougher than this!"

"Any idiot can survive the physical punishment of Ranger school," he answered. "This is different. The emotional pain is too great. You can mask it, call it something else, drown it with booze, but it keeps coming back up. I'm not going to be able to put your cowboy back together."

The emotional roller coaster that ensued in the weeks that followed this conversation as he moved back in, moved out, moved back in, and then moved out were further evidence of his spiritual confusion. In fact, he cited spiritual reasons each time he moved in the direction of obedience. Even so, each time he would succumb to the grip of sin and addiction. The grip it had on him was powerful.

The men who tried to help him and executed spiritual discipline all purposed to treat him 'as a gentile and a tax collector', once it became clear he was not going to turn from this path. This meant no contact. They based this on Matthew 18:17b

> *"...and if he refuses to listen even to the church, let him be to you as a Gentile and a tax collector."*

This bothered me for a long time. God pursues us. God leaves the 99 to go in search of the one missing sheep. If we're to be Jesus with skin on, shouldn't they have stayed in touch? From the standpoint of this woman who loved this sinful man, even though the marriage was over, it felt to me that all of God's people and even God had abandoned Steve in his hour of greatest need. In one of his letters to me several months after I moved back to Colorado, Steve also expressed a feeling of abandonment by his Christian brothers. As I prayerfully considered my response to Steve about this issue, God brought to mind many instances where his Christian brothers tried to be there for him. Some were before I left Ft. Bragg and some after. This is what I wrote on April 18, 1998.

> *As for your Christian brothers Steve, I want to share a different perspective with you regarding what went on in terms of them reaching out to you.*

> *I know that Pastor O called you for weeks last summer and you wouldn't return his calls. I know that Scott S got in touch with you, but you wouldn't meet with him. I know that Pastor H came to see you several times, but you wouldn't talk to him. Jason stopped into the unit to see you a couple of times, but you wouldn't talk to him either. Jason got wind that you'd been drinking one night this*

winter and were planning to drive to Ft. Bragg. He begged
me to give him your number so he could come get you.
I refused, as I knew you wouldn't let him anyway. Gina
and Jason found out you'd checked yourself into detox.
Jason made phone calls until he found out where you were
and was planning to come see you. I talked him out of it
because I was concerned it would be disruptive to your
recovery.

I also know that Vern called you about a week before
you went into detox. He waited for you at the restaurant
for 45 minutes until he got the call you weren't coming.
Vern and Chaplain B were both there for you. You made
it clear to all of these people you didn't want anything to
do with them. They wouldn't condone or validate what
you were doing, so you wouldn't listen to what they had
to say. You physically ran from Chaplain B to avoid him.
What did you expect these people to do? They did the
only thing they knew to do. Leave you alone. They were
not going to force themselves on you. They respected your
right as an individual to make a choice."

God is a gentleman and He never forces himself on people.
In Matthew 8:34, after casting the demons out of the swine, the
townspeople begged Him to leave.

"And behold, the whole city came out to meet Jesus; and
when they saw Him, they entreated Him to depart from
their region."

The next verse shows Him getting in a boat and leaving.
Christ respected their wishes. As I considered my concern that
his Christian brothers abandoned him, I began to see that they

not only followed the instructions given in Matthew 18, but they were also following Christ's example. These godly men were very Christ-like in respecting what Steve's wishes. It might not have been what he needed. But it was what he wanted.

The Vision

The question I couldn't resolve was this. Where was God for Steve in this crisis? So, at the suggestion of a creative, godly man, I asked God this question. I knew where He was for me. I could feel God's presence daily, in fact moment-to-moment. I have pages and pages in my journal of love notes from God in how He provided for me, led me, taught me, and guided me through this unfamiliar territory of divorce. In tough times, I clung to the Dennis Jernigan's song, 'If I could Just Sit With You Awhile'.

"If I could just sit with you awhile. If you could just hold me. Nothing could touch me, though I'm wounded, though I die."

Every time I played those words, I could feel the Lord's arms around me, comforting me, indeed, holding me, protecting me. I was a wounded child of God and He held me close through the darkest hours of my crisis. It was in fact Dennis Jernigan himself who suggested I pray for a vision of where God was for Steve in the trial. I attended a concert he held at a large church in Colorado Springs in the fall of 1997. He gave that challenge during the concert.

I prayed for months for God to show me where He was for Steve. The answer was slow in coming. I persisted in my prayer. I *needed* to understand. I *needed* to know. The image came to me one day, out of the blue. I was considering a difficulty in my life that had nothing to do with my failed marriage and suddenly, there was the vision, the long-sought answer to my prayer of where was God for Steve in this.

In the vision, I was with God, or more correctly, He was with me. I was hurting, crying, my body language downtrodden. I was sitting crossed legged on the floor. My head was down. My shoulder length blonde hair hung down, hiding my face. My arms lay on my legs, palms up. Even though the emotional pain was clear, I was open to God. My aura – the spirit I exuded was dark – depicting my sinful self. But God was there. He glowed and emitted light all around himself and me. I was enveloped in the light. It warmed me, comforted me, and gave me peace. I was often told right after Steve left me that it was so obvious I had peace in the midst of my pain. In fact, many said my face glowed. After the vision came, I knew the glow on my face was God's glow shining through me and the peace was his close presence.

In my vision, God had His arms stretched open so that more of His light would surround me. He was standing over me, on my left, protecting me and loving me, but He wasn't looking at me. His head was turned, looking back over His left shoulder towards my husband. As God protected me, my husband, whose being was dark like mine, was walking away from God. He was looking back over his right shoulder in my direction, but his gaze was fixed on God as he walked away from the protective circle of God's light and into the darkness.

It was as if God was saying to Steve, "My son, you are welcome to walk back into my light and protection. You are my child, and this is where you belong, but if you choose not to, I am going to protect this woman from the worst of your choices. She is choosing to stay and I'm going to wrap her in my love and light."

This vision was given to me in early September – a full year after I arrived back in Colorado Springs, at least ten months after I started asking God to show me where he was for Steve and a few weeks before my divorce was final. At long last, I understood that God had not abandoned Steve. God had pursued Steve. God had used the godly men who exercised church discipline with Steve to try to save him from himself in a sense. They had not abandoned him either. Quite the opposite. They had been obedient to execute biblically based spiritual discipline. Steve chose to walk away. He chose to walk away from grace, from God, from his marriage, his friends, his life.

A Battle Lost

A few weeks after God gave me this beautiful vision of love displayed for me AND for Steve, the divorce papers arrived in the mail. I simply needed to sign them in front of a notary. I called a local bank and asked how much they charged to notarize a document.

"Two-dollars," was the answer.

I drove to the bank. I sat in my truck and sobbed. I couldn't go in. I tried to call a couple of friends to pray with me. No one answered. I drove out of the parking lot and drove around for a few minutes, still crying…and praying. I went back to the bank parking lot. I still couldn't go in. Here's the thing. Signing those papers meant satan won the battle. The most difficult thing I've ever done in my life was to give that evil SOB the satisfaction of winning. He successfully destroyed a marriage, an Army career and the life of my soon-to-be-ex-husband.

In this moment, God reminded me of what one of the pastors in Fayetteville told me when I was questioning God's position on divorce as a believer. He mentioned 1 Corinthians 7:15.

"But if the unbelieving partner separates, let it be so. In such cases the brother or sister is not enslaved. God has called you to peace."

While Steve was a believer, the pastor admonished me that he was acting like an unbeliever and if this is what Steve wanted, I shouldn't stand in his way.

After a full hour of battling, I dried my eyes, blew my nose, re-applied my lipstick, gathered the divorce papers off the seat of my truck, walked with purpose into the bank and located the notary. Five minutes and two dollars later, I had done what was necessary on my end to be a divorced woman.

Word came from my attorney a few weeks later the divorce was final October 5th. On October 10th, a brisk Saturday morning, I gathered most of the cards and letters Steve gave me over the years, a coffee can, a lighter and our wedding bands. I drove my truck up Rampart Range road to the spot he proposed to me. I burned the cards and letters in the coffee can. Finally, I took the wedding bands and threw them down the side of the mountain. The day he proposed to me, in that very spot, Steve proclaimed so boldly that our love would stand forever, just like that mountain. It seemed only appropriate to leave the symbols of our love with the mountain, to hold for eternity.

Epilogue

There is something I want you, the reader to know. Sober Steve is a great guy. He's kind, courteous, thoughtful and romantic. Addiction brings out the worst in people. Sober Steve was a great teacher. During our short marriage he taught me to swim. I still swim today. He taught me how to shoot his .22 when we were living out in the country near Colorado Springs in case I needed to shoot a predator. He taught me 'righty-tighty, lefty-loosey'. That goes through my mind every time I turn a screw. He taught me 'it's always easier to pull than push." I still think that when I must move something heavy.

During our time at Ft. Bragg, I decided to compete in a mini triathlon. He helped me train, get the right equipment, and on race day, he helped me change in between legs. Mind you, he was a few weeks post op from an ACL repair. He stood, on crutches, in the North Carolina heat for four hours to be there for me, help me and root me on.

The last Christmas we were together at Ft. Bragg, found just the two of us celebrating alone. He planned the entire day. It was perfect. We sang carols, opened gifts, prepared Christmas dinner together, and ended the day making love in front of the Christmas tree. The thoughtfulness and planning he put into the day was very romantic and quite special to me because he wasn't a big fan of Christmas.

This is the guy I met and fell in love with. The other guy I talk about in this memoir is a stranger. In one of his letters to me after we separated Steve disclosed that he had been diagnosed with major depression and anxiety. In a phone call, he told me the doctors were looking into whether or not he was bi-polar. In addition, I have a letter from his mother telling me he was diagnosed with PTSD. He was in a lot of emotional pain and was self-medicating.

Two weeks after the divorce was final, I bought a house. It was a small starter house, but exactly right for me. I met a great guy three weeks after God released me from my marriage. We celebrated our 21st wedding anniversary in 2020. I never was able to have kids but have raised and loved four wonderful huskies. (Not all at the same time! We're a two-dog-limit house). My second husband is named Steve. Makes things quite easy in an argument. In my defense, his nickname is Gator and that's how he introduced himself to me. Lucky he did. I would have never gone on date one if I knew his name was Steve.

Our marriage is no different than any other. We've had many challenges over the years and will likely have many more. God has been faithful through it all. A friend reminded me of Psalm 37:4-6.

"Delight yourself in the Lord; And He will give you the desires of your heart. Commit your way to the Lord, Trust also in Him, and He will do it. And He will bring forth

your righteousness as the light, And your judgement as the noonday."

I hope my story has helped you and encouraged you in even a small way. "This is From Me" is my story, from Him. I pray you are blessed by God's provision and protection of me as He walked me through the most difficult chapter of my life to date. To God be the glory.

Dear Reader,

I would be negligent if I didn't share with you how to come into a loving relationship with Jesus Christ. I can't imagine going through this crisis you just read about with out the Lord loving me, leading me, growing me, guiding me, pursuing me, providing for me and protecting me. I am a sinner and don't deserve the grace He extends to me hour by hour and day by day. Romans 3:23 tells us "For all have sinned and fall short of the gory of God." The consequence of that sin is death, eternal separation from God. Those who don't look to Jesus to rescue them from that separation will spend eternity in a place where there is weeping and gnashing of teeth; a place often referred to as hell.

That's the bad news.

The good news is while we were still knee deep in the muck and mire of our sin, God made a way for us to be rescued. "But God demonstrates His own love toward us, in that while we were yet sinners, Christ died for us." Romans 5:8

Jesus became the sacrifice needed to cover your sin and mine, once and for all. But there's more to it than just Jesus dying a horrible, ugly and painful death on the cross for you and me. He overcame death and was resurrected on the third day after His burial! He's alive my friend!

It's hard to imagine the God who created the universe wants a relationship with you. He does. There's nothing you can do to earn His love and grace. It's a gift to you. In fact, He even gives you the faith to believe! "For by grace you have been saved through faith; and that not of yourselves, it is the gift of God; not as a result of works, so that no one may boast." Ephesians 2:8-9.

Rescue by Jesus is right there, at your fingertips for the taking. But you just must receive it. "If you confess with your mouth Jesus as Lord and believe in your heart that God raised Him from the dead, you will be saved." Romans 10:9

Once you've done that, you're a new creature in Christ and an adopted child of the Most High God. "Therefore, if anyone is in Christ, he is a new creature; the old things passed away; behold, new things have come." 2 Corinthians 5:17 and "But as many as received Him, to them He gave the right to become children of God, even to those who believe in His name." John 1:12

He has already chosen you. He already loves YOU. Will you choose Him today?

Humbly,
Audrey Joy

About The Author

 Audrey (Wyatt) Shrive is a West River, South Dakota, farm and ranch raised gal. Her parents, Russell and Betty Wyatt, instilled a strong work ethic, ability to problem solve, resourcefulness and self-reliance into the four children they raised. Audrey is a self-described over-achiever and control enthusiast.

These characteristics, along with a strong faith in Jesus Christ, her Lord and Savior, got Audrey through the difficult rejection and loss of her first marriage through divorce. The story of God's provision and protection during that tumultuous time is told in the pages of this book.

Audrey is a graduate of Hot Springs High School. She began her collegiate career at Chadron State College in Chadron, Nebraska. She then transferred and ultimately graduated from the University of South Dakota with degrees in Mass Communication and English. Audrey was a non-profit professional in the early part of her career working for Junior Achievement, Youth for Christ and the Boy Scouts of America (BSA). In 1998 Audrey was the first female scouting professional to be hired at the Pikes Peak Council, BSA in Colorado Springs, Colorado.

Audrey made a career change into the Insurance Industry in 2001. Working with a fortune 200 company, Audrey has been blessed through the Lord's provision and hard work to be a consistent top producer in her market. She even has a smattering of national awards under her belt. Audrey and her husband, Steve, work together in their insurance business. They live and work in Colorado Springs, Colorado.

Audrey and Steve are active in their church and host a weekly Bible study in their home. They enjoy the Siberian Husky dogs they raise and are both avid football fans, although, they don't agree on teams at all.

Audrey enjoys gardening, canning, reading, and writing. She also plays the alto saxophone in a community band.